ART IN COINAGE

THOMAS SIMON'S "PETITION" CROWN
FOR CHARLES II (p. 188)

ART IN COINAGE

The Aesthetics of Money from Greece to the Present Day

By

C. H. V. SUTHERLAND,
M.A., D.LITT.

*Student of Christ Church, Oxford
and Deputy Keeper of Coins
at the Ashmolean Museum*

London
B. T. BATSFORD LTD

For
MONICA

First published 1955

PRINTED AND BOUND IN GREAT BRITAIN BY
WILLIAM CLOWES AND SONS LTD, LONDON AND BECCLES,
FOR THE PUBLISHERS
B. T. BATSFORD LTD
4 FITZHARDINGE STREET, PORTMAN SQUARE
LONDON, W.1

PREFACE

ANY attempt to trace the fine history of art and design in the coinage of the Western world must be beset by difficulties. Coins have been produced in massive quantities ever since early Greek days. Many have been of exquisite quality: many more, indifferent or bad. Amid so great a flood of material, comparison is not easy. Often it is a matter of individual taste; and one man's choice will not be another's. And sometimes individual taste is swayed by fluctuations in fashion, as when one generation conceives a love for primitive style, and another revolts from it. Therefore, in singling out what appear to me to be admirable examples of coin-design, I have followed the only possible guide—the sense of spontaneous pleasure and the reasoned satisfaction which they have given me.

Some of these coins, even among the most ancient, are the work of known masters. But the great majority, are of unknown authorship—a fact which gives them a curious interest of their own, as it sharpens the critical sense in the recognition of style and in its attribution to the influence of dominant schools of design in every age. For each great man in every age there are many disciples on a lower plane; and the contribution of great artists must surely include the ability to inspire the lesser ones with the desire to imitate. The profusion of coinage at all periods thus offers an infinitely varied field for critical comparison, and few of those who are not afraid of looking at small things could fail to find there, in abundance, what will excite their interest and satisfy their taste. So far the attention paid to art in coinage has been small, or at least restricted. Greek coins, and Italian medals too, have for long claimed their devotees. And the coins and medals of Great Britain have naturally attracted a more than passing

7

interest in their own land. But study should go further than this, and the pleasure can be much wider. For coins and medals can be looked at so easily. They can be bought. They can be handled in great public museums at home and abroad. Their designs can be looked at in a wide variety of excellently illustrated books.

Many of the pieces which are discussed or illustrated in these chapters are very rare. So, too, in painting or sculpture what is most conspicuously good is often (and for many different reasons) rare. But this is not always the case. Artistry in coinage is not confined to a handful of world-rarities, and age after age supplies relatively common groups of coins in which the general standard of design is astonishingly high. Rarities, when their artistry is pre-eminent, do no more than exemplify the best in splendid isolation.

My main concern has been with coins rather than with medals. But medals are a deeply interesting and important by-product of monetary art, and indeed the mutual influence has for a long time been strong and intimate. Medals have therefore been discussed when that mutual influence has been specially noticeable or fruitful. In the recent past the study of medals, together with their own quality, has declined. Yet the emergence in our own day of medallists of great skill and imagination suggests that medals may become, once more, fit to claim the attention of connoisseurs and that their qualities of design may again influence the design of coinage in the right direction.

I have given much thought to the photographing of the coins and medals illustrated in this book. Each piece has been photographed direct from the metal, thus preserving to the utmost the liveliness of surface and tone which is wholly lost through the medium of a plaster cast. And in the great majority of cases the image has been enlarged above its natural size—most often up to $1\frac{1}{2}$ diameters, but occasionally up to two or even three. I have not been concerned to enlarge any piece up to sensational dimensions, for, although enlargement up to eight or ten diameters is often practicable, it

8

remains true that progressive enlargement, however revealing in some ways, transmutes and even impairs the essential quality of the original design. It is therefore necessary to compromise between the need for enlargement (for clarification) and the danger of impairing, or distorting, the original design. Nor have I hesitated to illustrate, on a single plate, coins which have been enlarged in different proportions, since one coin will take a degree of enlargement which in another coin is quite unsuccessful. In all cases the scale of enlargement is stated in the Key to the Plates (pp. 213 ff.).

For extreme skill and patience in the matter of photography I have to thank Miss Godwin, of the Ashmolean Museum at Oxford, and Miss Tweedy, of Fine Art Engravers, Ltd., in London. Each has produced admirable photographs, capable of very fine half-tone reproduction. My thanks are due also to the institutions or persons (specified in the Key to the Plates) who have allowed me to illustrate their coins and medals (sometimes in the form of fine electrotypes) or have themselves supplied photographs: for this latter kindness I am specially indebted to Dr. H. A. Cahn of Basel (Nos. 43, 44, 71–4, 82) and to the directors of the coin cabinets of Paris (Nos. 27, 52, 54), Munich (Nos. 9, 12), and of the American Numismatic Society in New York (No. 62).

C. H. V. S.

Cumnor, Oxford
November, 1954

9

CONTENTS

11

LIST OF ILLUSTRATIONS

LIST OF ILLUSTRATIONS

The tail-pieces of Chapters I–IV and VI are reproduced from Guillaume du Choul's *Discours de la religion des anciens romains*, published at Lyons in 1581 ; that of Chapter VII is reproduced from an engraving in a volume presented by John Whiteside, Keeper of the Ashmolean Museum, to Thomas Hearne in May 1722, and now in the Ashmolean; that of Chapter IX comes from the *Metallick History of the Reigns of King William III and Queen Mary, Queen Anne and King George I* (London, 1747), being plates prepared for Tindal's continuation of Rapin's *History of England*.

14

CHAPTER I

Introduction

COINS, considered as an art, possess a strong and indeed growing claim upon the keen eyes and the sympathetic interest of those who love what is beautiful. Viewed simply as a sequence of artistic creation, beginning in the seventh century before Christ, the coinage of the western world presents a fine and consistent continuity, combined with a perfection in survival, which perhaps no other art-form could surpass. Judged from the narrower, if more exacting, standpoint of purely technical achievement the record is scarcely less impressive—especially if medals are admitted (as they should be) into the company of coins, to which they are first cousins. At nearly all times coins have shown direct-ness of appeal, essential humanity, and a quality which, falling happily short of sophistication, rises far above the merely simple. For the art expressed in coinage is a pre-eminently social art. The first purpose of coins is to serve as a social commodity—the hard cash designed for the practical everyday business of hand-to-hand exchange. According, therefore, as they have been issued at a time when religion, commerce, wars and politics have been uppermost in national consciousness they have at most periods reflected the spirit of their time with a bright and curiously spontaneous fidelity.

This would not mean, of course, that art as expressed in coinage need have become at any time a great art. And it is perfectly true that at certain periods its standard has fallen to an undistinguished or frankly dull level: technical skill, for one reason or another, can quickly decay and—far more dangerous—political pressure or the frozen hand of conven-tion can cramp experiment and kill inventiveness. It remains

15

an undoubted fact, however, witnessed by many periods of brilliant conception and execution, that the general record over twenty-five centuries has been a noble one. Moreover, in one respect especially the study of coinage is unusually kind. For the coins—and the medals—of most ages exist in comparative abundance. Anyone who wishes to follow their long history, to study their flexible development, to enjoy their subtle combination of complexity and simplicity, can do so with ease.

If, in spite of this, the art-history of coinage has been to some extent neglected in the past while that of painting or sculpture or architecture has thrived, a reason is possibly to be found in the very small scale of the coins themselves. "The art of the miniaturist" is a phrase often heard in connection with the visual arts. Generally the expression has a faintly disparaging flavour, seeming to imply that a small work of art, however elaborate, however skilfully wrought, is some-how less remarkable, less praiseworthy, and even less difficult or exacting than a large one. Such a view must surely be misleading and false. The scale of a work of art, indeed, must be a most important element in the final balance of its total quality. But scale is not good or bad, pleasant or unpleasant, in itself absolutely: it is good or bad as applied to a particular object created for a particular purpose. We criticize a building which seems obviously too small or too large for its setting—and the rebuilding of the City of London round St. Paul's Cathedral is a sharp reminder of this question of setting, from which New York, with its dominant vertical emphasis point-ing to the limitless sky, is mainly free. A public statue which menaces its environs or is lost in them: a vase or a jug so large that it cannot conveniently be used for its natural and intended purpose: a painting which, however fine, cannot be so hung that its fineness is appreciated—it is not difficult to think of examples of miscalculated scale. Indeed, scale is as often a matter of practical convenience as of any purely aesthetic canons.

Reasons of practical convenience have brought it about that, for twenty-five centuries, coins (as distinct from medals and special pieces) have not normally exceeded a diameter of 1¾ inches: the majority lie well below that size. The designs which have been elaborated in each succeeding age to fill that tiny field deserve as much praise or blame, in their own right, as larger works of art. For the artistry which goes to the designing of a fine coin is beset by difficulties. First, there is the matter of spatial setting. A good architect should know the spatial setting most likely to provide him with the correct and most successful limitations to his work. Thus the Radcliffe Camera at Oxford rears its beautiful dome in the midst of a closely confining quadrangle formed by buildings of the most varied form, height and style, to none of which it does violence. The good sculptor is equally well aware of the extent to which the element of space will set off what he creates. Even such very small objects as miniatures proper or little jewelled toys like the works of Fabergé enjoy a stability in space by being specially displayed in some deliberately advantageous way—on a wall or bracket or elegant little table. But for a coin there is no such stability in space. Coins are never still for long at a time. Their primary purpose is to serve social and economic necessity; and to do this they must move—as they have always moved—steadily through space and time, not being displayed as *objets d'art* at all. They are absolute in themselves: their only spatial element lies in their own internal ratio between that part of the surface which is covered by design and that part which is left free. Their art-form is as self-contained as any in the world.

In addition to this essential aesthetic problem there is, secondly, a group of technical difficulties. Coins are produced (or, to use the proper term, "struck") by the pressure of two engraved dies upon a metal blank which lies between them. Today, indeed, the doubtful benefit of machinery, fostering the interests of economy rather than those of art, creates dies in untold numbers, reproducing them automatically from a large master-plaque which the designer has moulded in relief. But down to the middle of the nineteenth century the designer

17

of a coin was usually also the craftsman who gave his design reality by personally engraving, or at any rate finishing, the actual dies from which the coins should be struck. Carving dies of specially hardened metal: using instruments which, however good, were far removed from the precision instruments of the present day: working his tiny design in its actual size and taking care that it was neither so complex and "undercut" as to clog or damage the die when in use nor so low in relief as to run the risk of imperfect impression in the comparatively imperfect minting methods of the day—these were the tasks which the artists faced and overcame during the long centuries of greatness, achieving in addition the success of creating free-standing designs of great quality.

A coin which is not only pleasing to the eye but also practical as an object of exchange is thus created jointly by an artist's sense of design and technical mastery. Countless generations have excelled in this difficult art. And although modern coinage seems often to reflect the inherited tradition only dimly, partly through the application of mechanical processes and partly through the enervating weight of convention, the skill of contemporary medallists in many countries shows that the sense of design at least is still lively and experimental and that our own time is capable of producing work of equally matched freshness and beauty.

CHAPTER II

The Greek Artist's Vision

TAKE any random coin from the purse or pocket today. On one side it will show, in portrait form, the pictorial symbol of national sovranty. The other side will display, in one or another varied form, some badge or device strong in national association. These elements, which are now so familiar that they are automatically expected and accepted without question, are descended from the conventions elaborated by the Greek city states from the seventh century before Christ and onwards. If they are compared with the idiom of Muslim coinage through the ages, with its reiteration, in non-pictorial form, of religious dogma, or with the conventions of the Far East, which restricted the eloquence of a coin to a written statement of its issuing authority, its place of origin and its value, the contrast will be obvious and strong.

Even when that contrast is appreciated and established, we still have to discount certain qualities in modern coinage if we are to relish fully the excellence of what has gone before it. Modern coins present an absolutely circular form. Their edges are raised, like an unbreakable barrier around the designs they enclose. This barrier is strengthened by a severely circular band of lettering. Within this fence appears a design in a relief so low that at no point does it rise above the level of the raised edge. Let the imagination make certain changes, taking away the regular circularity of form, discouraging the raised edge, abolishing the constraining band of lettering, and increasing by three or four times the height of the relief in which the designs are shown. If the imagination can go so far, if the mind can clear itself of all that is associated with a

19

mass-production appearance, if we can consciously abandon the utilitarian conventions to which we are so strongly habituated, we shall be ready to understand and to enjoy the bold, free formula to which the best of the Greek coin-designers worked. For them there was little convention. They invited the observer to see on their coins no more than an image highly, if simply, wrought; individually conceived; isolated momentarily in space and time, though often lacking any confining border; splendid in its combination of freedom and compactness.

Chance and circumstance perhaps joined in helping to create such a free formula. In the prehistoric days of Minoan and Mycenean Greece metal plaques and ivories had been skilfully engraved and carved. And long before Greek cities began the daring experiment of designing a true coinage, to replace mere barter in metal, personal seals had been cut in the regular course of civilized life. An age without locks and keys demands an alternative safeguard, such as the use of a seal to preserve and proclaim ownership. Those who possess a signet ring today can see for themselves that a seal-impression is, as often as not, a design which exists freely in space. When they "lock up" their letters by impressing a spreading pool of wax, the impression of the seal has no more setting than the hollow in which the relief of the design stands. There can be very little doubt that the ancient art of engraving seals was the true origin of engraved dies for coins. When Polycrates, tyrant of Samos in the sixth century before Christ, was bidden by Amasis of Egypt to decide "which one of his treasures he would be most afflicted in his soul to lose, and, seeking . . . found he had a signet which he was accustomed to wear, enchased in gold and made of an emerald stone . . . the work of Theodorus, the son of Telecles of Samos," and cast this into the deep sea, he sacrificed his indubitable badge of ownership and authority. Throughout many centuries afterwards the relationship between seals and coin-dies was intimate: in the Middle Ages, especially, the design of a country's "great seal" was essentially that of

GREEK CITY-BADGES

1 Eretria (p. 33), 2 Rhegium (p. 33), 3 Metapontum
(p. 27), 4 Athens (p. 26), 5 Elis (p. 33)

GODDESSES OF GREEK CITIES

6 Athens (pp. 27, 45), 7–9 Syracuse (p. 28)

many of its coins. In early Greek days, indeed, such a relationship was very natural, since money was often minted from
metal safeguarded in temples, and was issued, as it were,
under the seal of the god or goddess concerned. The very word
"money" is derived from the word "moneta", epithet of
Juno "the adviser", in whose temple the earliest Roman
coinage was produced.

So, just as the marks engraved on a seal showed the ownership of anything it impressed, the marks engraved on a
coin-die showed by whose authority the money was coined
and were, so to speak, a monetary seal. A little set of coins
made at some Greek city (Ephesus?) east of the Aegean
showed the device of a stag, around which, in Ionic Greek
characters, appeared the inscription "I am the badge of
Phanes." It is uncertain who Phanes was: the word may be
the epithet of a goddess, or the name of some rich merchant
or trader. Nor does the question greatly matter, for these
primitive pieces assert the authority for coinage in the seal-
like fashion which was to characterize the whole subsequent
family of western money. And, with the immemorial idiom
of the seal-engraver transferred to the making of coin-dies,
the way was open for the employment in die-cutting of that
same free style which had always been a feature of seals.
This link, indeed, would have been all the stronger because of
the close relationship which existed between engravers, metal-
workers and sculptors. That same Theodorus, son of Telecles
of Samos, who had made Polycrates' ring was engraver,
metal-worker, sculptor and architect: among other works he
"cast his own portrait in bronze at Samos, famous not only
because of the marvellous likeness but also because of the
minuteness of the work—the right hand held a file and the
left held, in three fingers, a tiny four-horse chariot . . . so
minute and wonderfully wrought that a fly, made at the same
time, covered the horse-team, the car, and the driver with its
wings." The story—and it may be no more—illustrates all
the elements which went to make up artistry in early coinage;
and Theodorus was but one of many artists who, in the days

before pre-eminence spelt fame in a single specialized medium, worked with equal skill in many fields.

Greek coinage began in earnest about 650 B.C. Before that time money had consisted of small, rough lumps of metal which were crudely impressed with a punch. But once the art of die-engraving was adapted from that of the seal-engraver, the progress, though slow at first, was steady enough, moving along lines which became more and more strongly sculptural. A sculptural treatment of coin-designs means, of course, that these designs were made to appear in comparatively high relief. The Greeks were an essentially rational and highly practical collection of peoples: they knew, as well as we know, that coins once circulated quickly become rubbed. Even so they chose, almost without exception, to have their coin-designs executed in a relief so abnormally high that we should consider it "medallic", in the modern sense of the term. And perhaps they were right. A pocketful of modern coins, lying flatly side by side, rubbing each other over the whole area of their faces, appears to suffer very little less abrasion than affected the high-relief coins of the Greeks, on which the design normally rose to its greatest height about the centre of the coin, and which took much of the burden of wear on their thick, irregular edges. In any case the Greeks were content with an idiom which allowed their die-engravers full opportunity to employ the skill in sculptural and plastic forms for which they showed such general aptitude. Nor were they deterred by the fact that dies deeply cut for high-relief coins wear out far more quickly than dies more shallowly engraved. Modern coinages are subject, above all, to the scrutiny of those whose job it is to avoid expense; and it is perfectly true that the 60,000 strikings which the Royal Mint obtains from an average die would be much reduced if those dies were more deeply cut. On the other hand, the Greek technique produced a coinage which still arouses the wonder and admiration of each successive age.

The Greek engravers, then, were not unduly restricted by any civic dictates of consciously enjoined economy. In making dies for coinage they were able, from the first, to work as sculptors in a miniature field; and they succeeded in grafting —in a curiously effortless way, seldom matched and perhaps never excelled—the sculptor's idiom upon the technique of the cutter of seals and gems. From this was to arise the peculiar beauty, the specially choice perfection of Greek coinage. One question only remained. What subjects were the artists to represent when they carved their dies?

Their world was young—it had scarcely settled into anything like stability after the prodigious upheavals of an age of abrupt movement and multiple colonization. Their imagination was fertile and free: they worked in a field totally unembarrassed by the binding force of any former traditions. In only one respect could they receive dictation. In most Greek city-states coinage quickly became a regular, usually an annual, affair. Its production, in pure metal and of proper weight, was the responsibility of a city's financial officers and was all the more important in those states which, like Athens, Aegina, Corinth, and certain cities in Thrace and Macedonia, controlled rich mineral supplies and used their coinage to market the resultant metal in made-up, "trade-marked" form as a staple export. It was very important that the devices of such coins should speak clearly of the cities which issued them: this same cardinal principle has operated in all later coinages of a similar kind—the gold and silver poured out in the great days of the Spanish empire; the central European pieces of Joachimsthal silver, which gave a name, through "thaler", to the dollar; the silver coins of Mexico today. So the die-engravers of Greece were normally required to represent either the distinguishing badge of the city concerned or—what sometimes came to the same thing—the head of its protecting god or goddess. These limitations were not rigid: they allowed the utmost freedom of interpretation; and when, as sometimes happened, there was a cessation of a city's coinage for a few years its resumption was usually marked not so much by any attempt to "modernize" former design as by its more fundamental transformation. From these

25

simple precepts, lightly imposed and freely followed, arose the combined variety and beauty of Greek coins.

City-badges were equally simple and apt. Some of them were essentially religious—the head of the god or goddess or some sacred object with local associations. Others were commercial in character, representing a city's staple product in terms of agriculture, pottery, fishing, or mining. And some expressed the religious element through myth or other local allusion. The civic badge of Athens' coinage—apart from the head of Athena herself—was the owl (4), the bird which has for ever haunted that city and was associated, through its appearance of sagacity, with the sagacious goddess Athena. This owl, small, squat, its head alertly turned to confront the observer with its great eyes, was perhaps the most famous city-badge of its day. It stood for a coinage of unsurpassed quality and value, the praises of which were celebrated by the dramatist Aristophanes. Opposite the Peiraeus, port of Athens, lay the barren island of Aegina, which supported a population far in excess of its own natural capabilities by the vigour of its sea-borne trade. For more than two hundred years the coins of Aegina were marked with a sea-turtle, which abounded then, as it does now, in the waters around its rocky coast—a creature sacred to Aphrodite, and perhaps suggesting that the temple of Aphrodite guarded Aegina's mint-treasure as Athena guarded that of Athens. After Athens finally conquered Aegina, her bitter foe for years, the sea-turtle, lithe and smooth in its free element, was later replaced by the land-tortoise.

Beyond Aegina, again, on the Peloponnesian isthmus, stood the strong and famous city of Corinth, where (so the story went) Athena helped Bellerophon take and tame and bridle the winged Pegasus who, alighting on that barren citadel, caused water to gush from the rock by a blow of his hoof. And Pegasus became and long remained the coin-badge of Corinth, rivalling but never surpassing the commercial fame of the Athenian owl. To the north of Athens lay Boeotia, where the badge of the shield symbolized the safely banded confederates of the Boeotian League. Looking west to Magna Graecia we can see the sea-crab and the Mediterranean fish which the French now call the *dorade* as the twin badges of Sicilian Acragas. Of Italian Metapontum, now a waste of sandy scrub, it was recorded that its citizens "so prospered in farming that they dedicated a gold harvest at Delphi"—no doubt a golden sheaf of those barley-ears of which one alone, ripe, shining and magnificently upright across the diameter of the coins, furnished the city's natural badge (3). Other cities, too, used natural products to mark their coins: those of Sicilian Selinus bore the wild parsley leaf, *selinon*, the abundance of which gave the city its name, and African Cyrene chose to picture the silphium plant—an elaborately beautiful botanical form—from which she earned so much of her income.

These few examples, chosen from among scores, must serve to show the simplicity of the normal Greek city-badge, rendered with a clarity which seldom called for any explanatory inscription or name. If the head of a god or goddess or hero was required on a coin, either to supplement the city-badge, as at Athens, or ultimately to take its place, the choice would have to come from a narrower circle. Athena and Apollo were perhaps most commonly represented, and this was doubtless because the characteristic qualities imputed to them were so closely connected with the everyday run of human life. Athena (who did not belong to Athens alone, though Athens claimed to be her most favoured shrine) was the goddess of intellectual wisdom and armed strength (6): she was clever, gentle, and confident in her virginal powers. Apollo (13, 14) was the god of manhood in his prime: he was the sun-god (23), who could make all things grow or wither: he was the god of healing, of song, and of prophecy, as kindly to those he loved as he was terrible to his enemies: sternly beautiful, as on the Olympia pediment, vibrantly strong, or softly gracious, as the imagination suggested. Besides these, Zeus the fatherly sky-god, Hera his consort, and Aphrodite, the goddess of love and fertility, who needed no adjuncts to identify her universally pervasive charm, are frequently seen, together with Dionysus (11), the wine-god reveller who protected all vineyards, Hermes the slick, sly traveller (12, 17) and Heracles who, more than human and yet less than divine, played the ancient role of universal redeemer from toil and tribulation. In addition to the great gods and the heroes there were the innumerable local divinities, like Taras at Tarentum (16), and spirits of great antiquity who dwelt in river or fountain or marsh—gods and nymphs always potent. These were always to be courted and reverenced, like the clear, strong fountain of Syracusan Arethusa (7–9), and sometimes to be feared in time of flood, like the rushing bull of a river at Gela near by (18). Arethusa's head is sometimes shown slight, gay and dainty, sometimes fuller, heavier and more powerful, as if to emphasize the silent force of the clean water welling up. The man-headed bull of Gela's river softens gradually as men learn to control the monster, and at length confesses their victory.

A Greek artist required to interpret subject-matter of such a kind upon his coin-dies would do so strictly according to his social and political environment and within the tradition in which he had been trained. The Greeks were not a nation. They were a collection of peoples, of interwoven stock, living in independent groups, city by city, each deciding their form of government, each making their laws, each with their deeply conceived sense of sovranty. From the resultant interplay of influences a perceptive artist would feel himself bombarded by an astonishing variety of style and idiom. Many flourishing artistic traditions could exist simultaneously; and each of these could be absorbed and reproduced well and badly—by the good and the inferior artist working literally side by side, as the coins show them often to have done. But among all this variety, and beset by so many variant and exciting influences, the artists who designed Greek coins showed one characteristic in common. The Greeks as a whole were naturalists. Not, however, in the sense that they were lovers of nature, or inspired by what is called the romance of science. They were not attracted by nature in the broad sense: they did not care

GODS OF GREEK CITIES

10 | 11
――――
12
――――
13 | 14

10 Aetna (p. 46), 11 Naxos (Sicily) (p. 46),
12 Aenus (p. 46), 13 Amphipolis (p. 48),
14 Catana (p. 48 f.)

ADVANCES IN GREEK DESIGN (I)

15 Acanthus (p. 36), 16 Tarentum (p. 28), 17 Sybrita
(p. 37), 18 Gela (p. 28)

to observe the total natural scene, however dear its associations might be: by contrast with the Romans they were uninterested in landscape—even the sickle-shaped harbour of Sicilian Zancle, conceived as if from an aerial view and studded with warehouses along its sides, is symbolically filled with a great dolphin to suggest the depth of its anchorage. What the Greeks saw with absolute clarity and loved to reproduce with utter faithfulness was the single object—man or beast; bird, fish, or flower; or even a man-made thing like a shield or a pot or a lyre or a wheel. To such observed objects as these they brought the greatest degree of penetrating analysis. And, by doing so, they contrived to set them in isolation. They saw these things as they were, by themselves; and that, of course, is the reason why their studies of birds and fish and grasshoppers are identifiable studies. Analysis never became romantic: still less did it lead, as it often leads today, towards the artist's self-analysis of his own emotions. The objects which they themselves looked at every day, absorbing them entirely and delineating them in total isolation, can still be looked at daily on the coins without any fading of their power or persuasion. Because the artists expressed the fullest quality of beauty, intellectually felt, in what the senses observed, these men achieved the idealism which is the hall-mark of classical Greek naturalism. If naturalism is frowned upon today it may be partly because the ideal is not so strongly or persistently sought.

But simple naturalism, however intensely infused by idealism, could have left the art of Greek coins as forbidding, as dispassionately cold, as the works of the nineteenth century classical revivalists, dedicated to form and not to feeling. There is more in the world than the purity of aesthetic truth and beauty intellectually approved. To restrict art to these essentials is to reduce life to the level of a specimen for analysis and dissection—or rather, to reduce living; and the living of life is more important than life itself. The Greeks were well aware of this. They knew that humour cannot be neglected, that life contains much downright ugliness, and that ugliness often becomes amusingly grotesque. And in all this they took appropriate interest and delight. The early Acropolis sculptures of Athens writhed with fantastic monsters. On vases we see a comic galaxy of dwarfs and oddly shaped old men who remind us still that there is a human norm. Greek literature gives us caricature, whether in Aristophanes or Theophrastus; and on the coins themselves it is possible to gaze, in wondering horror, upon the superbly ugly Gorgon's head which had once turned its beholders into stone, or to watch satyrs stealing away unresistant maidens in happy obviousness.

With all this there was a love of what was brightly decorative—a love natural to a people living in the brightness of the Mediterranean climate where the sunshine, free from mist, renders all forms harder and stronger and brings out colour as a natural relief. Buildings and figures of pure and shining marble were picked out, or even more lavishly adorned, with brilliant reds and blues—four hundred years ago the same colours were being beautifully applied in stained-glass windows and painted ceilings and effigies—and this natural decorative instinct was strengthened by the influences transmitted through Asiatic Greece from the art-forms of more ancient civilizations. From here came the idiom of pattern, familiar in the pottery of eastward-looking Corinth, the arrangements of flowers and rosettes, the ribbon-like bands of animals and beasts formally opposed as in modern heraldry. The island cities of the Aegean, lapped in an isolation of limpid air and water, tempered this eastern extravagance and exuberance. For them it was possible to see single objects in utter clarity and yet invest them with a decorative quality. The art-forms thus filtered westwards, constantly differentiated and cross-fertilized, to be diffused in yet new forms in mainland Greece, Italy and Sicily, where their ultimate and highest elaboration was achieved.

Such, in general, was the setting in which the Greek engravers of coin-dies approached their problem—the sculptural representation, in seal-like form, of an immense variety of city-badges of religious or geographical significance. Some of these badges have already been mentioned, and there are many more, some naïve, but many of them splendidly successful as freely decorative designs. The lion's mask, by the accident of enforced emigration, travelled westward from Samos to become the coin-badge of Italian Rhegium (2). It confronts us head on, and eye to eye, so that, combined with the wrinkled skin of the nose, the furrowed forehead and the whiskers upturned to echo the curve of the coin's edge, a lively and grimly humorous effect is gained: a lion keenly observed and deeply pondered. In the island of Euboea, the city of Eretria used the device of an octopus (1). Above the squat, bulbous body and head the eight great tentacles wave, curled four this way and four that, a design reminiscent of the marine subjects loved by Minoan artists a thousand years earlier. For Olympia, Peloponnesian shrine of Zeus, there was the stupendous eagle's head (5). Dr. Charles Seltman has remarked of this design how rarely an artist has achieved the task of suggesting a kind of divinity in an animal form. Its impressiveness derives alike from its strictly observed accuracy, its masterly engraving, its sombre control of a piece of metal which has no border—no other element, indeed, than the small white-poplar leaf used to symbolize the earthly setting of the temple in its sacred grove.

Here, to quote but a few, were badges of unforgettable quality and emphasis. In their own day they were part of the heraldry of the times. For the modern world heraldry spells a conventionally fixed and frozen design, with vigilant experts ready and skilled to criticize the smallest inaccuracy or variation in the formula. It is true that, in the Greek world too, deliberate adherence to a conventional design was occasionally preferred. The famous Athenian owl (4), for example, was "frozen" in the archaic form in which it had been conceived: like Maria Theresa's equally famous dollars, still coined annually in millions with their original date, the "owls" had won world markets in Egypt and the Middle East which were much too valuable to be jeopardized by any change of design, and so the city which led the world in its artistic standards, Pericles' "school of Hellas", was also the city which immobilized her coinage-style where it stood in her years of adolescence. But elsewhere there was general desire for change: the essence of the badge might be preserved from year to year, but its presentation could be infinitely varied. Of all the countries today it is difficult to find any which enjoys such flexibility in coin-design or such a willingness to make great changes, not so much for the sake of change itself as for the chance of major improvement.

CHAPTER III

The Greek Maturity

THIS desire for change in itself, as a means of attempting fresh and varied interpretations, can best be seen in the great range of coinages which Greek cities—large and small, and some known only from the coins they made—poured out in the fifth century before Christ. Thus the Pegasus of Corinth, in its early form seen gliding to earth, now stands or walks or soars to the sky. Gela's river-god, the bull with a bearded human head (18), which we have seen softened and submitting to be crowned, is transformed into a beardless youth (20). He is grave and intent: his short hair lies flat, bound by a diadem, like that of the famous bronze Charioteer of Delphi. And, again like the Charioteer, his jaw is full, rounded and a little heavy, suggesting the power of the god—power indicated no less by the concentration of expression in the eye and also by the little horn which rises above his forehead, the symbolic link with his earlier bull-form. At Syracuse the coins had from the first shown a racing chariot; for Syracuse, the wealthy, was the home of many who could afford this most costly, most exciting and most heroic form of sport. The earlier coins show the chariot drawn by two horses, walking quietly (22): later they gallop, when the engravers had mastered the problem of the horses' legs, all superimposed in plane upon plane of relief; and then, in the grand climax, the two galloping horses were increased to four, their flying hooves filling the field of the coin with the orderly confusion of passionate effort (21).

The coins of Sicilian Acragas have been noted already for their device of a crab. But Acragas claimed and used a second badge as well—an eagle perched, lonely, often on a column.

35

Mute at first, and with its great wings folded, it later appears standing with its cruel talons fixed in the belly of a hare lying, upturned, upon a naked rock: now the wings flutter, to give the bird balance for his grim work, and the beak curves down for the attack. The final stage of elaboration is seen on one of the noblest of all Greek coins (24). Here the self-same eagle is joined by its mate which, likewise standing upon the defenceless belly of the hare as it lies kicking, its eyes staring in terror, screams in triumph with lifted head.

In certain parts of the Greek world conceptions of an altogether different kind were preferred and explored. The Greek cities and half-Hellenized tribes around the north shores of the Aegean lay somewhat apart from the main currents of thought and symbolism which prevailed in communities further south. Life in Thrace and Macedon was sterner and harder: there was wealth to be won from the mines and from horse-breeding, wine-growing and agriculture on the approaches to the great plains of southern Russia, but climate and conditions were less kind and the spirit, therefore, perhaps less sensitive. This seems to be reflected in the many *genre* scenes which the coins of this region display. Heavily built farmers walk beside their massive ox-wagons: maidens are rapt away, all unprotesting, in the arms of passionate satyrs: on the coins of Acanthus (15) a lion has leapt upon a bull, bringing it to its knees, and plunges its teeth in its haunch: at Mende we see, first, Silenus' ass alone, and then Silenus mounts it, lying carefree, back to front, winecup in hand. In Crete, too, an individual set of conceptions existed. Its cities were still stored with the dark force of old Minoan legend. The Minotaur himself still runs on the coins of Cnossus—a bull-headed man, so much more grim than the man-headed bull of Gela; his labyrinth— for all the world like a formal garden-maze pictured from the air—is also shown. Europa, seated in the crutch of a tree, dallies bride-like with the eagle whose shape great Zeus has assumed. The mints of Crete are full of stories of savage bulls and helpless maidens, their excitement undimmed after centuries of repetition. But the newer, younger Dorian gods were there too. Sybrita made coins of the utmost grace and delicacy, bearing a head of Hermes (17). The god is short-haired, youthful, with well-rounded cheek. On his head he wears, perched high, the wide-brimmed petasus or sun-hat appropriate to those who travel afar: in front of him we see his caduceus, the special wand which marked his character. Both in conception and in composition this coin must be ranked in the highest class.

There was, then, in the fifth century, a constant advance in conception; and this restless desire for what was new was controlled, and well controlled, by increasingly high standards of design and increasingly good technical method. It is salutary to remember, again, how new the art of coinage was. The coins elaborated and produced for the Coronation of Queen Elizabeth II were successors to a tradition which, from time to time, has used every apparent trick and explored every possible device. But for the Greek designers the field of experiment was still very wide: granted that such conventions as the use of city-badges had arisen, there was comparatively little to limit variety either in composition or in style. It is not easy to compose a satisfactorily balanced design within a circular or roughly circular outline. The emphasis may be mainly vertical, as on the coin of Metapontum (3), or mainly horizontal, as on that of Sybrita (17), with its emphatic hat. Or it may be found in a circle within the circle, like the lion's mask at Rhegium (2) and the continuously writhing lion-bull group at Acanthus (15). Alternatively the artist may work on the system of an angle within his circle: such, essentially, were the forms of the Athenian owl (4) and the eagle-head of Elis (5). Or he may seek the more powerful effect of directional planes deliberately opposed, such as the sternly right-angled opposition used with such success in the scene of Gela's river-god being crowned (18) and of the two great eagles at Acragas (24). Choice of emphasis may, indeed, seem wide; but for an engraver who was reluctant to do the same thing twice, and whose output must nevertheless be large, it must have appeared uncomfortably small. There were, of course, certain minor tricks which he could play with. He could make his design without any border at all, or with a border of lighter or heavier kind. He was free to distribute his lettering as he wished—if (that is to say) he was required to incorporate lettering at all, since for long years many mints relied solely on their badge to show the coin's authority. Thus Athens included the first letters of her name as a stylistic foil to the little owl (4), and Sybrita spaces the name of its citizens up to the left and across the top of Hermes' head (17) —an inconspicuously effective balance to the caduceus in front of it.

It was perhaps by some accident of technique that the tyranny of the circle was lightened. Certain mints—that of Athens was among the first—appear to have found it more convenient to use a square die, of relatively small size, with which to punch the reverses of their coins. The object of this was almost certainly to displace as great a volume as possible of the central area of the metal, driving it more powerfully into the ever-increasing depth of relief on the obverse die. From the earliest times the obverses, or "heads", of Greek coins had tended to show designs in very high relief, mounded to the centre of the coin, and with the increasing adoption of portrait-designs the same general effect continued. The introduction of the square reverse-punch to serve a technical purpose also helped to solve the problems of pure composition for those for whom design in a free circle was difficult or unwelcome. To set a square within a circle is to equip yourself with a useful set of clear angles and parallel planes as a harmonious basis for further elaboration. Moreover, the "square-punch" coins had this additional advantage: they provided a natural ground-line on which figures could stand or sit or walk, and made it unnecessary to employ the device of the "exergual line" which can be seen, for example, below Britannia (141) on every penny today. Even so it may be doubted if the "square-punch" technique in fact encouraged designers to their greatest work: the men who chose the

ADVANCES IN GREEK DESIGN (II)

19 Peparethus (p. 42), 20 Gela (p. 35),
21, 22 Syracuse (p. 35)

GREEK MATURITY

$\frac{23}{\frac{24}{25}}$ 23, 24 Acragas (pp. 27., 35 f., 45 f.), 25 Panticapaeum
(p. 55)

aesthetically harder task of placing a balanced composition freely within a circle almost certainly produced the finer designs. Their problems were to be recognized, and again solved with brilliance, by the medallists of the Italian Renaissance.

Advances in conception and in the theory of composition were matched by advances in technical skill. Not, however, as the result of any sudden improvement or extension in the range of instruments which a die-engraver used. His tools were those which, in general, must have remained the standard kit for metal-engravers for centuries afterwards: a graver's wheel, ordinary drills of larger and smaller size, a blunt or knobbed drill for excavating the larger depressions (such as the main area of a human head or a body), a burin and perhaps a compass. The wheel and the ordinary drills probably took the main share of the work. With these simple tools, adequate in themselves for engraving the specially hardened metal of the dies, the artists trod the confident path leading to their more and more skilful use. The first half of the fifth century before Christ was for Greece a time of swift and stimulating development. A single heroic decade had seen the defeat of Persia and of Carthage. The power of Greek cities increased: commerce multiplied: wealth accumulated; and new markets for economic expansion were sought. It was a time of self-confidence, of spiritual revolution and indeed exaltation, in which men turned their backs to the past and looked only to see what could be extracted from the future. As a result new styles were introduced and perfected in the various fields of art. In particular the die-engraver turned, quite surely, into the artist who could cut sculptural dies. Their coins, continuing the high relief so well loved since coins began, became much more complex in design: the demands made upon plastic skill were extraordinary, with plane piled upon plane and figure upon figure. The rate of progression had been, by any standards, wonderfully swift, and for that very reason the Greeks made a legend of those who, not so very long before, had given that progression its first impetus. It was small wonder that, as we learn from

41

Pausanias, the first connoisseur whose writings have come down to us, the earliest "Daedalic" works were invested with a kind of reverence, as if there was something divine dwelling in them; for those primitive creations, the first to show open eyes and parted legs and outstretched arms, had broken away from the stiff and often lifeless forms inherited from Egypt and the East, and no one now knew, still less remembered, the superbly fluid and decorative idiom which had made a glory of Minoan art until the collapse of Cretan power a thousand years before.

The fifth-century artist's first problem lay in the three-dimensional representation of the human body (19). This most subtle and continuously flowing form, whether represented frontally or from the side, must be made to suggest what lay round the corner, out of sight, as certainly as we know that the stripe on the painted barber's pole will return and confront us again. Ten or fifteen years after 500 B.C. this problem was being solved satisfactorily; and then it was time to pay attention to the greatest problem of all—the representation of the human face. Here the difficulty was not one simply of three-dimensionalism. The essence of the human face is the expression which infuses it from the mobility of eyes and mouth. Hitherto, if the eyes were widely opened to their limits, and if the mouth was extended into the upward curving lines of a seeming smile, it was felt that sufficient expressiveness had been achieved: the subtleties of eyelids, of the shadowed eye-socket, of rounded yet firmly set lips, had seldom been examined. When, therefore, convention began increasingly to favour the appearance on coins of the heads of gods and goddesses and heroes and local spirits, the die-engravers who multiplied these portraits year by year found themselves the necessary exponents of a rapidly expanding form of plastic art—the portrait in relief.

Too much, of course, can be talked about the *mystique* of portraiture. But its achievement on an exalted scale in any civilization is worth a moment's consideration, and the achievement of the Greek die-engravers is as remarkable as any other. In making the likeness of a divinity and giving it individual and humane character they were often making a radical departure from traditional, "old-style" representation. Thus, when the Aeginetan sculptor Onatas was commissioned, early in the fifth century, to replace the Phigaleans' cult-statue of Demeter he found that the original image, which had been destroyed by fire, had shown her "in form like a woman except for her head: she had the head and mane of a horse, and forms of serpents and other creatures sprang from her head." We read that Onatas, partly as the result of discovering a former painting of the original image, "but chiefly, as the story goes, by visions revealed to him," made a new bronze image, and it is not to be doubted that those "visions" were in fact the comprehension that Demeter's likeness must at length be modernized and expressed in the proper terms of his own generation. Onatas indeed was only doing what Athens herself did when, after the occupying Persians had cast down the sixth-century statues of Athena's maidens, she preferred to see new figures set up, contemporary in style and feeling, rather than to resurrect the old.

But, quite apart from the deeply felt necessity of representing old and traditional divinities in new forms, the engravers had other important points to consider. To put the head of a god upon a coin; to centre attention on that isolated head alone, with whatever distinguishing attributes he thought it right to add; to give the portrait a universality, matching the world-wide emphasis of the city-badge on the other side, and yet an individuality, which should shine through those traditionally ageless, unlined features, sleek and rounded: here were problems indeed. It was one thing to set a solid statue in a shrine: Quintilian, for example, recorded of Pheidias' vast Olympian Zeus (perhaps seven times life-size) that its beauty seemed to have contributed something new to religion, for the very grandeur of the work matched the grandeur of the god. It was quite another thing to represent godhead in miniature, with no shrine, no religious setting, no vast three-dimensional majesty to awe the spirit. Nevertheless the effort was made and, to modern eyes at least, with sure success.

For a considerable time the coin-designers attempted profile portraits only. This, while being technically expedient, was perhaps also natural. The image of a god would confront a visitor who entered his shrine: the devotee could look directly upon it, with an immediate and personal sense of worship. The profile portrait suggested a difference, the essence of which is hardly diminished in the profile portraits of kings and queens today. Profile enabled the observer to see the god without being seen: he could, so to speak, steal up beside him—not to take improper advantage but simply to make the act of identification independently of the act of reverence. To put a portrait on a coin is to immobilize the likeness for every moment it is observed: between such moments its urgency is lost. It was as if the god passed in procession, looked at in a sudden moment and not worshipped in extended and personal intimacy.

Thus the earlier profile portraits designed by Greek die-engravers—and they were all of deities, heroes and spirits, and never of living or even historical persons—were conceived in a simple, clear and dispassionate way: formal, perhaps, and suggesting a certain remoteness. It could almost be added that these early portraits showed a lack of eye-to-eye contact with the observer, but that would not be true. Artists did not at first make their coin-portraits truly three-dimensional. Their planes of relief could not successfully suggest that for every plane seen there was, so to speak, another just round the corner, waiting for the observer to walk round and look at it. And indeed it is perfectly true that the human eye, in profile, is extremely difficult to represent. Viewed frontally it offers no great problems, but, seen from the side, the eye-socket begins (but only just begins) to turn the corner—the cause of our being able to command a sweep of vision, however imperfect at the extremes, of over 180 degrees. The early die-engravers were unable to surmount the difficulty of suggesting this undoubted three-dimensional fact in two-dimensional idiom. Or perhaps, after a time, they became careless of its existence and willing to perpetuate an old convention. In any case they designed profile portraits in which the eye was shown frontally. This feature of archaic Greek art is as natural and convincing in its idiom as it is important for the chronological analysis of coin-portraits and relief-sculpture as a whole, for in the fifth century the formula of truthful representation was quickly realized and universally applied. On the modern observer the frontal eye in the profile portrait exerts a far from unpleasing effect. These passive, placid portraits are irradiated in a curiously graceful manner: it is as if you approach for a sideways glance at the god, who then notices you by a sudden sideways flicker of the divine eye.

Coin-portraits of the gods were not named, though the name (which frequently appeared) of the city or citizens that produced a coinage often served to identify the portrait if this did not fall into the class of universally recognized conceptions. Differentiations were in any case meticulously observed, and subordinate adjuncts helped to "fix" the identity of the portrait quite unmistakably: the gods were, so to speak, accurately "typed." The Athena who wore the close helmet surmounted by a brave crest, together with ear-ring and necklace, was Athena Parthenos of Athens (6) and of those many other cities—like Thurii, Naples and Velia in Italy—which for political or economic reasons acknowledged the same protection. The Athena who wore a deep-bowled helmet, its face-piece tilted up and back to show her graceful features, was Athena Chalinitis of Corinth, great commercial rival of Athens and mistress of a colonial empire where the same representation was accurately followed. Zeus is bearded, full and venerable, as befits the great father of gods and men: his consort Hera, much more than a girl, much less than a middle-aged woman, is distinguished by a flat embroidered cap or *polos*. Apollo was the essence of young male godhead in its prime (13, 14). His innumerable representations differ in a number of respects, but there is seldom any hesitation in recognizing him. Often his hair is long to feminine degree, appropriate to the god of the Muses. His features may be noticeably full and rounded; and upon his head he will usually wear an elaborate wreath of the laurel that was sacred to him. But in his expression there is always the note of superhuman majesty and inner strength. With his lips firmly set and his eye steady, with the abundant beauty of his hair laurel-crowned, he conveyed to the Greeks at one glance the mystery of a life in which sunshine, song, healing and prophecy took chaste and undisputed place above all other elements. Not that the other elements were neglected. The female portrait, deliberately unadorned except by simple ear-ring and diadem, is Aphrodite the goddess of love, who needs no adornment. Dionysus, the wine-god, is bearded but not old (11): a wreath of ivy-leaves binds his thick hair: his lips are full, his eye half-curtained by its heavy upper lid. How different was Dionysus from Silenus (10), whose image meets us on one of the most splendid of all Greek coins. For him, too, the ivy-wreath, but riding high above his ass's ear on a bald pate: for him, again, the beard, but framing lips coarsely protruding beneath a squat nose and a large, burning eye—animal as opposed to divine lust. Hermes the traveller was distinguished by his two travelling hats, one cap-like, close and brimless, its edge adorned by a row of studs (12), the other wide-brimmed against the greater heat (17). And Heracles, who among his labours overcame the Nemean lion, wears by right the lion's skin head-dress which marked his place in the pagan world as man's redeemer by toil and danger—a role in which earthly kings were later to cast themselves (55, 56).

In such ways were gods and godlike beings differentiated, primarily by their distinctive attributes and forms and then, as time went on, by an expressiveness of feature that was in each case appropriate. The course of the fifth century B.C. brought with it an increasingly rich conception of human effort and human rationalism. Gradually the Greeks came to feel that the gods were less remote and more like themselves—more truly moulded, indeed, in the human image. Accordingly, the divine portraits changed their character. Humans of divine form now, gods and goddesses and heroes and nymphs—at length given a true profile eye—look steadily ahead of them and show whatever mood, whatever emotion is suitable. Usually they are calm, confident and strong, as every city liked to think itself in an age of nascent imperialism and cut-throat commercial rivalry. But some of the cleverest engravers were not content with this, and in many cities they took the supreme step of making the portrait full-face or nearly full-face, infusing the features with the fullest measure of concentration or even passion. These are no mere representations of the old gods enshrined: they are gods in human form who have left their shrines to face the world.

The success of facing or semi-facing portraits on coins and medals is generally a matter of dispute. Technically the execution of a fully facing portrait is probably no more difficult than that of a profile: a three-quarter portrait is doubtless very much more difficult. Contention arises rather on aesthetic grounds. A coin is made to circulate, and circulation will rub it, flattening the nose and thus destroying the carefully designed balance of the features. And although such spoiling of the balance can be minimized by various means—the broadening of the hair-masses, or the addition of a helmet to the head—the fact remains that a worn facing-head portrait is unpleasing to look at. On a medal, of course, which is not intended for circulation, no such damage is caused and the original planes of relief are preserved. Even here, however, the frontal idiom has not gained much popularity. There is an essential and deeply felt difference between the profile portrait, which seeks to express no direct relationship, conveyed emotionally from eye to eye, between the observer and the figure portrayed, and the facing portrait in which that emotional contact is immediately perceived. And on the whole the objective appeal of the profile has far outweighed the subjectively felt compulsion of the facing head.

But there can be no doubt that many Greek die-engravers from 450 B.C. onwards were increasingly interested in the new possibilities of the facing head. It was tried in a good many cities—at Syracuse and at Catana in Sicily, at northern Amphipolis and Aenus, at Ionian Clazomenae and in Cyrene and Rhodes. Moreover, it is beyond question that the facing-head idiom added immensely powerful variety to the guises and emotions in which godhead could be represented. We have already seen in what different ways the character of Apollo could be suggested by profile treatment. Two facing heads, each of the utmost technical perfection, display the differences with redoubled emphasis. Thracian Amphipolis broke away from the domination of Athens' empire in 424 B.C. Steeped in the artistic traditions of Athens, now at their peak of excellence; wealthy from the proximity of rich silver-mines, and so able to employ first-class artists; and proud in the enjoyment of political independence, Amphipolis within a few years issued a coinage of full classical magnificence. The three-quarter portrait of Apollo (13) shows rounded forms— the lips soft, the cheeks almost heavy, the upper eye-lid a little drooped, the lower lying full. The hair waves and curls, neither neat nor exuberant: at one side its mass is considerable, serving the purely technical purpose of relieving the nose from the full pressure of rubbing in circulation. Though the general effect is one of gentle grace there is no effeminacy: this is Apollo the artist, as sweet in song as he was swift in his heavenly course. With this conception we may compare that of the artist Heracleidas on a noble coin of Catana (14), made about the same time. Here Apollo is thinner, and looks stronger. Though the lips are full the forms are harder, and the sideways inclination of the head lacks the peculiar appeal achieved at Amphipolis, where the effect is that of a god deigning gently to turn. But the Apollo of Catana is not gentle at all. His eye burns fixedly upon the beholder: his hair, its profuse curls confined by a laurel wreath about the crown of his head, falls in the thin, shimmering waves of a mirage on either side of his face. This is Apollo the sun-god,

48

conceived in all the heat of Mediterranean Catana: a god of immense power, yet calm and undefiled.

A mere two centuries had elapsed since Greek engravers began to experiment with coin-portraiture. The brilliance of its swift development brought about a great and natural change in the status and reputation of the artists themselves. At first they were regarded as mere city-craftsmen—men of skill, indeed, but not of fame—who were employed in a medium not easily to be regarded as comparable with that of the sculptor or painter. But the impact of sculptural technique upon the engraver's art, and possibly also the influence of painters in the matter of composition and design, led to results so fine and conspicuous that, in an age when sculptors became internationally famous, like Myron, Pheidias and Poly-cleitus, die-engravers too acquired a world-wide fame which is reflected by their signing of their dies. The names of several are known. Recorded at first in abbreviated form, at a time when the signing of dies was obviously a new practice dis-creetly tried, they were later written in much fuller or even complete form. Heracleidas' signed die for Catana (14) has already been noted, and other artists as well left their name on the coins of this city—Procles, Choirion and (21) Euaenetus. This last was one of a number of brilliant engravers of pre-eminent quality whose services were sought by the great city of Syracuse. With Sosion, Eucleidas, Phrygillus, and—perhaps the most remarkable of all—Cimon, he designed dies in a tradition of nobility and magnificence which has for centuries past made the Syracusan coinage famous. Some of these artists worked elsewhere too; for example, Phrygillus, who carved dies for Greek cities in Italy. And there were others of equal merit: Polycrates and Myr . . . at Acragas; Da . . . (5), Po . . . and Olym . . . at Olympia; Theodotus at Ionian Clazomenae.

Their signatures sometimes appear quite boldly: at Clazo-menae, for instance, the relevant coins proclaim "Theodotus was the maker." But often it was the case that, the greater the artist, the greater was his ingenious sense of fancy in placing his name inconspicuously in more or less microscopic letters, sometimes so small that their existence was not noted until comparatively recent times: for work on this minute scale it cannot be doubted that lenses must have been used, made of rock-crystal. Written large or small, however, and in full or abbreviated form, these signatures argue that from the second half of the fifth century B.C. the art of coin-design had become internationally famous. Moreover, the beautiful designs of the foremost artists attracted the compliment of imitation in cities, often far away, which admired these masters without being able to bring them long distances, at heavy expense, to give their own coins the latest touch of elegant perfection. For there was no copyright in conception. A new treatment of the portrait, in profile or full-face, could become the property of the whole Greek world, by admiration and sedulous imitation, as much as any new conception by sculptors such as Alcamenes or Praxiteles. And thus these great coin-designers, who had come for the first time to work in something much wider than local or regional traditions and thus had evolved what was an international style, could see that style yet more fully internationalized by the influence which their work exerted all over the world.

For every artist now known to us there were, of course, scores at work of whom the names can never be known. Many of these were engravers of the highest quality: even more were men of average capability, who sometimes, in a moment of special inspiration, achieved some outstanding conception; some, too—and the coins themselves, considered and compared by the hundred, show these to have been naturally the most numerous—were men whose conceptions were undistinguished and sometimes even banal. It would be a great mistake to assume that the level of artistic vision in Greek coinage was universally high. In one respect, nevertheless, the standard everywhere *was* high. From a technical point of view there were comparatively few engravers who, from the late fifth century onwards, had not mastered the mechanics of die-engraving. Any city of any consequence at all could command the services of skilled engravers even if they were not artists of high conception. Thus the character of Greek coinage began to change in the fourth century. Technical facility can easily dissuade its possessor from effort; and without effort experiment is not easily undertaken. Moreover, the Greek world of the fourth century was itself a world of changing standards. An age of action was giving way to one of philosophic analysis and reflection: as the works of Plato and Aristotle attest, men were no longer interested in action alone, but were equally inclined to ponder the questions of what they had been doing, and why. These factors are seen as a strong influence on Greek art in general. It was not yet academic, though mere technical facility, giving the universal power to imitate at will, was moving it in that direction. But it began to lose some, at least, of that sense of the ideal which had previously distinguished so much of the best Greek work.

These very circumstances, however, opened up one more great field of artistry in coinage. Portraiture, hitherto pitched to a divine level, became humanized. The latent power, the restrained intensity, which had characterized the fifth-century representation of divinities was now to give way to the passionate emotions of man himself. Sculptors like Scopas and Praxiteles set a new fashion, making the features of their statues display human emotions: they "infused the stone with what the soul feels," and were not any longer content to create what depended, for its full emotional value, on the observer's reaction. Thus, not only was divine portraiture humanized, as when Praxiteles represented Aphrodite "with a *disdainful* smile playing gently over her parted lips", but human portraiture in its own right was now explored. This at first was perhaps felt to be easier, or less subject to the dissuasions of convention, in the Greek or semi-Greek lands to the east of the Aegean. Here the political climate was redolent of personal power and despotism. The great shadow of the Persian Empire, the lesser shadows of Persian satraps and local dynasts, had for long accustomed men

51

to accept the phenomenon of absolute power in the hands of individual men—a phenomenon which Greeks of the mainland and of the west had spent a century in resisting. The individuality of kings and despots was therefore interesting in its own right and worthy of expression in portrait-form.

Of the Great Kings of Persia we have no portraits: it was enough for their coins to represent them as purely conventional full-length figures. But superb likenesses were made, at the end of the fifth century, of Tissaphernes (30), the famous Persian satrap of the maritime provinces of Asia Minor, with whom both Athens and Sparta flirted desperately to gain support each to vanquish the other. These portraits, minted in Greek coastal cities, would certainly have been the work of Greek artists. And these artists gave fresh proof of what the previous Greek coinages had proved—proof of the power to observe objects clearly in isolation and to reproduce them in the most sensitive plastic form. Tissaphernes is shown as a dignified, bearded man: he wears upon his head the Persian tiara, folded back flat from the forehead (for only the Great King himself could wear it standing stiffly upright) and draping the neck behind. His eyes are large, deeply sunk and shadowed, and powerful in their intensity: his nose is hooked and, considered with the lips which show below the drooping moustache, strongly expressive of cruel absolutism. The mastery lies in the antithesis between this burning, ruthless face and the soft folds of the tiara in which it is framed. For half a century the portraits of gods had shown "character": but this character took the form of qualities— such as grace, beauty, serenity, strength—which by their very universality fall short of suggesting the particular identity of this or that man. But, given distinctive features; given an expression which breathes just a little more of this or that quality than the average man possesses; given the power to arouse men's curiosity about man; and human portraiture at once begins.

Its extension to mainland and western Greece was slow, but in east Greek lands it was quickly learned, and the city

GREEK PORTRAITURE

GREEK AND HELLENIZED PORTRAITURE

29
30 | 31
32

29 Antiochus I (p. 56), 30 Tissaphernes (p. 52),
31 Bagadat (p. 57), 32 Antimachus of Bactria (p. 57)

of Cyzicus in northern Asia Minor quite plainly took ordinary people—old men and youths and maidens—as the normal models for the very varied figures which its lovely coinage represented. One particular old man posed for a portrait (26) which must be regarded as one of the very earliest to be made of such "ordinary" people. He was bald and bearded: old enough for his brow to be furrowed and the skin of his neck to be creased, but not so old as to be debarred from winning and wearing (for what actions we can only guess) a laurel wreath. The bald cranium is oddly square: the thick nose wrinkled at the bridge; and naturally full lips are pressed together in one of those mannerisms of constraint or patience which advancing years encourage or impose. In every sense this is the portrait of a man, free on the one hand from the universal quality which goes with godlike features and on the other from the slightest taint of caricature.

For early caricature we must go still further north and east, to Panticapaeum, a half-Hellenized city lying on the east Crimean coast. Panticapaeum was rich in the gold of the Urals and, though so remote from the main streams of Greek civilization, could plainly afford first-class artists of the finest Greek tradition. The three-quarter portrait of Silenus (25) which glares out from its coins in the middle of the fourth century is one of the Greek masterpieces. While the Silenus of Sicilian Aetna (10), a century earlier, had been the universalized embodiment of human lust, just as portraits of the gods embodied universalized virtue, the Silenus of Panticapaeum shows the particularity which is the mark of true portraiture. The wild hair, furrowed brow, swollen eyes, coarse nose and open, mouthing lips are taken from the life; and in the aggregate, assisted by the satyr's ears, they form something nearer to caricature than to portraiture.

The chance of portraiture came to Greece as a whole when, in the second half of the fourth century, she was swept up into the Macedonian monarchy of Philip II and Alexander the Great. But tradition was too strong and the chance was missed: the royal portraits were still idealized. Philip, bearded and senior, appears in a benign Zeus-like aspect: the young Alexander is represented throughout the Greek world as a beardless Heracles, with a lion's skin framing his passionately god-like features. Only in eastern mints, scattered through Asia and the Levant, was any attempt made to avoid this formula by imparting to Alexander's features some individual distinction; and none of these attempts achieved greatness. But with Alexander's death and the partition of his vast territorial empire fine portraiture again sprang up, most notably under the Seleucid kings of Syria. Seleucus I, indeed, is cast in an heroic, idealizing mould, with all that a beard and a laurel wreath can do to suggest the godlike stature of Zeus himself. For his successor Antiochus I (281–261 B.C.) the artists entirely changed the tradition and at once achieved a realism which was to become the most famous feature of Seleucid money. Beardless, like most of his successors in the dynasty, Antiochus is shown in all the pathos of human as opposed to divine power (29). The laurel wreath, heavy and decorative, has given way to a simple diadem, over which fall, in a studiously "naturalistic" manner, a few curling locks of hair rendered in a fashion which Alexander's die-engravers had first popularized. Over the low forehead the hair is rolled in and under; and, almost meeting this roll, the eye socket—large, heavily shadowed and arched grotesquely high—contains an eye which peers anxiously out. The expression is one of worried attention, and the feeling of strain is accentuated by the fine-drawn nostril of the long nose, from which springs a heavy furrow that leads down to frame a thin-lipped, tight mouth.

Greek portraiture had represented gods as admirable; but earthly kings were men, and men were interesting. Moreover, in an age when dynastic and internecine feud began to multiply, it must be a function of the coinage to show the true likeness of the lawful monarch. From such considerations arose the fine series of Seleucid portraits; worried or noble or gross or feeble, these kings were displayed with all the characteristics which would make them recognizable, and, when a reign was long, grow old before our eyes. The influence of Seleucid portrait-artists was felt far and wide, and by the second century B.C. astonishing "realist" portraits were being made by first-class Greek artists for royal courts, half-Hellenized, on the Pontic shore of the Black Sea and, thousands of miles away, in the regions bordering on India which the great Alexander had opened up and in which the Greek tongue lingered on as a polite reminder of the sources of the new culture. Portraits of Mithradates and Pharnaces of Pontus (28, 27), of Bagadat (31), and of Antimachus of Bactria (32) can take their place among the world's chief artistic works —the first two constraining coarse and heavy features to a regal dignity; the last looking out with the firm, quizzical eye of experience upon his kingdom, his aging head protected by a sun-hat.

Five centuries had passed since the earliest die-engravers had begun to design coinage. In that period they and their successors comprehended the whole of the art of coinage. By trial and error they discovered what could, and what would not, afford proper material for design in a miniature, restricted field. They succeeded alike in expressing a sense of the divine and of the human: in addition they could invest the inanimate object, or the beast or bird, with that celestial light, that utter isolation, which to the English romantic poet seemed in retrospect "the glory and freshness of a dream" but to the Greek was the pondered analysis of reality. Technically they quickly attained, and their leading artists for long preserved, the very highest skill, imparting to the image on a coin the full richness of three-dimensional suggestion by the use of bold and prominent relief. Greek coinage can show us many an indifferent coin, crudely conceived and executed in the early days, facile and academic in the later, and often undistinguished at all times. Considered as a whole, however, its general standard of perfection, through the combination of power and instinctively sought beauty, causes it to stand out from among the artistry of any monetary series of comparable length. What Pericles said of his fellow-Athenians, calling them lovers of the beautiful, disciplined in taste and naturally thoughtful without being effeminate, could be applied as a description of Greek artists, at their best, in general: they, like the Athenians, adapted themselves to the most varied forms with the highest degree of versatility and grace.

CHAPTER IV

The Development of Roman Portraiture

ROME, with a retrospective exactitude which was a part of her nature and a strong influence upon her art, religiously preserved the date of her foundation in 753 B.C. At that date Greek coinage had yet to begin, and Rome herself was to survive for nearly five centuries, using metal currency in bulk or bar form, before she developed a true domestic coinage. Like Roman art-forms in general, Roman coinage took a long time to mature. It started as an appendage to the coinages of older cultures. Greek art, in its Hellenistic phase, extended from end to end of the civilized world. Men, whether they lived in the Greek colony of Marseilles or the cities of the Black Sea, or under the rule of the Greek Ptolemies in Egypt or the half-Hellenized kings of distant Bactria, were confronted by a widely internationalized set of art-forms. In the hands of Greek artists and their skilful imitators, the subject-matter of Greek legend and mythology had become standard material everywhere. It is an easy temptation, in thinking back over Greece and Rome, to try to follow these two great civilizations each in a separate course, independent of the other. The truth is seen when it is realized that Rome was founded and developed in an almost wholly Hellenized world, in which, by about 300 B.C. (when Roman expansion was under way), Greek philosophers, scientists, poets, dramatists, artists, architects and orators appeared to have done everything that could be devised to render their medium brilliant and memorable.

Italy herself, along her southern and western coasts, was studded with many a town and city of purely Greek origin

59

and expression. In Etruria, the powerful and uncomfortably close neighbour of early Rome, there was to be seen a remarkable offshoot of Greek art, the significance of which is becoming more clearly interpreted; and there was an Etruscan coinage of Greek form and content. Thus when Roman coins first appeared in the third century B.C., at length displacing the currency of lump-bronze with which previous generations had made do, they were in form no more than one more Hellenistic addition to the money of a Hellenistic world. Nevertheless they swiftly developed distinguishing characteristics, which derived from special founts of influence. Of these Etruria was doubtless one: not for nothing had Etruscan kings been planted in Rome. Another influence was the personality of the Roman people itself in the comparatively early days before world-conquest had turned a small city-state into a vast, cosmopolitan centre of imperial administration.

The distinctions between Greece and Rome, Greeks and Romans, Greek art and Roman art have been exhaustively discussed and observed, often in laboured comparison. But the Roman essence deserves to be studied and appreciated in its own right. The Roman nature was severe, patient, practical and thorough. Politically it was conservative: in religion it was traditionalist. So too might many Greek communities have turned out (as iron Sparta in fact did, in disciplined isolation from her neighbours) but for the accident of the Dorian invasion, which set whole populations on the move just when their intellectual powers were in the ascendant, and but for the stupendous, little expected repulse of Persia and Carthage, which revolutionized the Greek spirit. Early Rome, however, remained comparatively free from such stimulating shocks. Unchecked, she could continue to show her genius in combining the steady absorption of neighbouring peoples, under her oligarchic leadership, with their indoctrination in a political theory which carefully defined the precise civic and legal status of the individual. Chary of experiment and distrusting philosophical speculation, nascent Rome set herself a single clear task. She was to extend—

under the protection of the old gods, and directed by statesmen of the old families—her own orderly civic system among her neighbours, using the forces of commerce, intermarriage and law at first, and later the force of arms if that proved to be necessary.

It is neither difficult nor fanciful to detect these general characteristics in her early coinage. This began, as we have seen, in a polished Greek idiom, with coins intended for commerce with Greek colonies in Italy. These were quite evidently designed by Greek artists: conventionally elegant— a tribute to the taste of those Greek markets which they had to win—they were fashionable without being inspired. But when Rome had conquered Carthage in the second Punic war and had thus established her clear position as mistress of Italy, her coins at once developed a purely Roman style, little affected by Greek artists or by any need to attract markets. This style was formal, dry and often stark to the point of harshness. It allowed designs to be represented, in annually unchanging form, with absolute clarity and conciseness. Such, too, had been the coinage of Athens over the many generations which preferred to make no change in its design; but the distinction was that, while the Athenian coins were rendered in a consciously archaic style by artists who, if they had wished, could have worked in the highest traditions of subtle plastic skill, the early Roman pieces give the impression of sheer indifference to the main problems which had stimulated Greek excellence in general to the art of coinage.

The helmeted head of Roma was executed in a conventional expressionless manner in strong contrast with the "intense", restrainedly emotional treatment long since accorded to Hellenistic portraits of deities. This was symbolism of the plainest and most practical kind. Equally practical was the mark of value which these coins bore—a mark clear and unequivocal, which contributed nothing to the total design and implied the existence of no exacting standards of aesthetic criticism. And the accompanying design—Castor and Pollux on horseback, or Diana driving a chariot—showed no greater warmth of feeling or love of technique. In one respect only did the early Roman coinage show technical advance, or rather conform to technical advance already made elsewhere. For the coins were neatly struck and well rounded: in other words, manufacturing processes were efficient and up to date. This was important, as the Roman coinage of the second century B.C. became in some senses a world-coinage owing to the steady extension of Roman rule by force of arms along the Mediterranean basin. The coins were struck in immense numbers by methods which demanded the technique of mass-production; and the key to mass-production lay in an efficiency which cut out wasted time.

For about a century, therefore, Rome continued to turn out coins which were banal. Technically they were un-interesting: the subtlety of engraving dies with delicately contrasted planes of relief was an art for which at this juncture no time could be found. And although the subject-matter of their designs fairly quickly began to show variety by the transition from religious myth to semi-historical legend, the treatment of the new designs showed no spacious-ness of conception. Among these neat, practical, sharply struck little coins there was scarcely a single one, over the space of three generations, which excites the aesthetic emotion of an even averagely good Greek coin. Often they were ugly: at their best they were seldom more than quaint; and they give no hint of the particular beauties which Roman coinage was in time to show.

Nevertheless influences were at work which were to affect the style of Roman coins very deeply. Roman skill in human portraiture has become proverbial, and is to be seen and enjoyed in sculptured portrait-busts from quite an early period. This skill derived from various causes. There was, for example, the strong tradition of later Etruscan art-forms nearby, in which portraiture (strong, sometimes coarse, but often successful) played an important part. There was the Roman habit of making a death-mask when the head of an

62

CELTIC ORNAMENT AND ROMAN REPUBLICAN
PORTRAITURE

ROME: LATE REPUBLIC AND EARLY EMPIRE

39 Vercingetorix (?) (p. 67), 40 Julius Caesar (p. 69),
41 Antony (p. 69 f.), 42 Pompey (p. 70),
43, 44 Augustus (pp. 75, 83 f.)

important family died: such masks were afterwards preserved and displayed in the house in order to emphasize a
family's lustre, new or continuing, in the political activity
which throughout most of the Republican period was the
pre-requisite of social prominence. Again, there was the
instinctive and peculiarly Roman appreciation of the personality of the individual, reflected in the whole basis of
Roman law, with its personal safeguards and personal respon-
sibilities. The person, in the legal sense, was all-important:
the personage, in the civic or political or historical sense,
was no less so. It is enough to reflect upon a contrast to understand the strength of this social idiom. Modern cultures,
inheritors of the classical tradition in its Roman interpretation,
feel a standard and universal interest in human portraiture
of all kinds: the Greeks, at their greatest and most splendid
period, scarcely indulged this interest at all and have left
us the merest handful of portraits, and then only of the greatest
men, from an age when great men abounded.

Accordingly, when changing times and traditions led the
Roman mint-masters to abandon the old, stock designs with
which Roman coinage had begun and to replace these with
designs recalling the historical events of the past, on which
the Roman mind at all times dwelt so fondly, they naturally
conceived the idea of placing on the coins portraits of the
great men of the past. This new development took place at
the beginning of the first century B.C. It was greatly strengthened by the increasing Hellenism of Roman culture. The
sack of Corinth half a century earlier had marked the final
downfall of Greece, and Greek philosophy, literature and
art-forms, carried to Rome by a growing band of teachers and
technicians who saw there the opportunities for a livelihood
which Greek decadence denied them, were being carefully
studied and absorbed indiscriminately. The impact of Greek
idiom and Greek technicians upon a Rome which by now
bestrode the Hellenistic world from end to end was the true
beginning of the characteristic excellences of art in Roman
coinage.

Late Hellenistic art itself had become academic. But the influence of Hellenistic artists and of universalized Hellenistic style upon the still parochial forms of Rome brought forth an art so profoundly hybridized that it could never become wholly academic. The political objects which Roman art had to serve—for the Roman mind did not favour art for art's sake, and the sentiments of Pericles' funeral oration were unthinkable at Rome—kept it flexible and varied. Thus versatile artists were ready to work in any tradition, pouring their utmost skill into portraits of different kinds and telling whatever story they were required to interpret. This story might be legendary, and calling for deliberate archaism, as seen in the treatment of the portrait of the Sabine king Titus Tatius (36). A masterpiece of imaginative retrospection, the head is rendered in a solid, uncouth style. The features possess a rustic nobility, expressionless as archaism demands. The beard is uncombed and falls in thick, shaggy locks: across the tall head, with its jutting forehead, the hair is combed straight and severely, its untrimmed ends forming a ragged frame for the face. This was a portrait over which some die-engraver worked hard. He may have drawn a traditional likeness from some sculptured representation of Tatius. In any case he was reluctant to produce what would be merely conventional, and his coins contain that essential quality which it is so difficult to define—the conception, well pondered, well wrought and strong, which isolates itself increasingly from contemporary work by other hands.

Other portraits of the same period breathe the same spirit of individual personality strongly felt and skilfully transmitted. All the traditionally civic virtues which amounted to Roman Republican statesmanship are set down in miniature in the dry, austere portraits of C. Antius Restio (37) and C. Coelius Caldus (38), both long dead when the coins bearing their heads were made in the middle of the first century B.C. Possibly we are here looking at likenesses derived ultimately from a death-mask. Caldus is represented as elderly. Furrows mark his brow, radiate from his eyes, and frame his mouth; and his long neck is skinny. But his hair (which we imagine grizzled, from its texture of short, close masses) covers his head, except where it recedes a little at the temple. The portrait is not by any means of first-class quality, for, though the modelling of cheek and neck are admirable, the nose is not truly modelled at all, the artist having been content simply to engrave its outline on his die according to earlier practice. Its power is nevertheless undeniable. Once more there is visible the phenomenon of a portrait in which it is obvious that the artist's feelings have been aroused, as a stimulus to technical skill.

Against the massively uncouth archaism of Titus Tatius and the dry realism of Restio and Caldus may be set a fourth portrait (39), in yet another style, made in the same period. Whether or not he is Vercingetorix, Julius Caesar's great adversary in Gaul, cannot be said, though it is easy to understand how the attribution could be made. For this bearded human head—it is no god—is un-Roman. Emaciated features, accentuated by the thinly twisting "imperial" beard, are topped by hair which streams sharply back in the rush of speed. Deeply hollowed eye-sockets express a sombre urgency: the mouth is set firmly. Around his neck he wears, as a badge of rank, a chain. Behind the head, which was carved eccentrically within the circle of the die and thus gives a fine balance to the composition, is placed a sharply pointed shield. Work such as this shows that there were artists living in the late Republic on whom the fine traditions of previous die-cutting, moribund in the second century B.C., were by no means lost.

These four admirable coins, made within a comparatively short time of each other, display many varied tricks of style and technique. Hellenistic and Roman usages, idealism and realism, live side by side. The intense interest which a good artist felt in the rendering of human features can be well judged by the designs on the reverses: in all four cases these are jejune—poor in conception and weak in execution. Human portraiture, raised to such splendid heights on the later Greek coins, opened up a field which exactly corresponded with the Roman outlook on life in a political society. With the question of style—whether a portrait should be rendered in the more emotional Hellenistic tradition, or with drier Roman fidelity—the average observer would not have been concerned. Thus it would have been possible for Greek artists to work side by side with Roman, each producing characteristic work, each borrowing and adapting the peculiar excellence of the other.

Roman coinage, by this time, was being produced in formidable quantities. The methods of minting, as is certainly known, were virtually unchanged from those of Greek days— the impact of a hammer upon engraved dies with a coin-blank laid between them: Roman coins themselves picture the simple apparatus, which is shown also in the murals in the House of the Vettii. Increasing demand for coinage, however, led to the necessity of multiplying die-engravers. And though in no single case throughout the whole vast sequence of Republican and Imperial coinage is the authorship of a coin-design known, it can be said without much doubt that at most periods good and bad work was being done simultaneously. It would not be surprising if, on the occasion of each major change of design, a master-die was cut by a master-engraver. From this, lesser engravers could work, incorporating as much of the spirit of the original as they were competent to do. Conditions such as these would help to explain what has often puzzled modern critics of certain phases of Roman coinage, namely, the difficulty of defining the style of a coinage at a given moment: so often it is uncomfortably varied even though the subject-matter of the designs may be, for the time being, stereotyped. Probably it would be right to reserve the term "style" for those engravers who made master-dies of obvious quality and authority: for those lesser artists whose task it was to multiply this pattern the term "treatment" is good enough. Those whose work consists of obligatory imitation can scarcely evolve style, which, correctly used, must surely connote a considerable degree of original and individual creation.

In Greece, die-engravers had sometimes been artists of

fame, but more often nameless, competent city-craftsmen. The Roman engravers, so far as is known, were always men of humble birth, freedmen or even slaves, frequently no doubt of eastern Greek origin: by the third century after Christ mint-workers had been impressed into a regular caste-system from which they could not easily escape. If at times there was a noticeable unevenness in the artistic quality of Roman coinage in the five centuries which followed its true birth in the late Republic that would be no matter for surprise. What is genuinely remarkable is that, over this long period, the nameless and socially humble engravers who worked at Rome and the many outlying mints produced so much that is, aesthetically and technically, admirable and outstanding.

Their principal contribution, of course, was the development of the portrait. If Julius Caesar had escaped assassination in 44 B.C. there is little doubt that the portraits which appeared on the coins struck later in that year would have been the first life-time portraits to be placed on the coinage of Rome. In all respects they introduce the long series of imperial heads which was to come thereafter. The representation was in the dry spirit of Roman realism (40): a spare, strong masterful likeness of a lean and sinewy man upon whose head rests the victor's wreath. There is no "intenseness" within the portrait itself: its success—apart from the fidelity of the features—comes from the observer's own reactions, which cannot be so wholly different today from those of a world in which Caesar's political and military career had for years been a byword. Political portraiture, once begun in this spirit, was immediately developed by the triumvirs Antony, Octavian and Lepidus. Antony commanded that eastern part of Rome's territories in which he chose to remain, the object of every breath of anti-Cleopatran slander which blew from Rome, and from which he derived solid supplies of men and money. His portraits preserve the fine tradition of the Seleucids and the Ptolemies. This versatile politician and military leader, so desperately traduced in his role as a Shakespearian lover, appears to us on the coins in all his gross strength (41). His great head, jutting chin and "heroic" tousled hair are represented, not in the Roman realist style, but in the eastern idiom, with an undercurrent of emotional passion charging—and justifying—the probable exaggeration of natural form. The posthumous portraits of Pompey the Great (42) on the Sicilian coins of his son Sextus are, on the other hand, of a more sophisticated style, with finer, bolder modelling and far greater delicacy of engraving. Here, once more, is seen the antithesis of treatment to which the contemporary die-engravers were subjected.

With the defeat of Antony, with Cleopatra, at the battle of Actium in 31 B.C. the Roman world began a new era under Octavian, soon to be known as Augustus. Total reorganization of administration included the coinage, which now began to assume a more uniform aspect. Henceforth the imperial coinage was deliberately adorned to serve a most practical end. Its purpose, as has been abundantly demonstrated, was to spread the imperial message year by year. The classical coinages of Greece had remained without any essential change in their symbolism for long periods at a time: their designs advertised the cities which produced them and, though they were constantly "re-styled", according to the fashions of the day and the taste of the artists employed, they did not seek to be eloquent in the sense of conveying political messages or propaganda. By contrast, the designs on the coins of the Roman Empire changed every year: often a single year would see the production of a dozen designs never used before, and elaborate care was taken, as each year passed, to emphasize the appropriateness of a design by making appropriate changes in dating. These coins were made to be looked at and studied. While those of Greece had borne no more inscription than sufficed, in combination with portrait or badge, to identify the issuing city or king, Roman coins left nothing to chance. The literate and illiterate alike were supplied with information in the form of complementary words and pictures. A man who could not read could at least sense the personality of an emperor from the highly individual, highly polished treatment of his portrait, and could comprehend the essentials of his policy and achievement from the simple and clearly conceived pictures which accompanied the portrait. The imperial coinage was a masterly tool used in the interests of imperial political philosophy. Circulating up and down the whole extent of the huge empire it preached, in each reign, the emperor of the day; and this was to preach Rome, for the emperor *was* Rome. The portraits and their accompanying designs would have fixed every eye on the man at the top of the imperial structure, not merely as the symbol of the system but as its living and powerful exponent, supreme in civil power, commander-in-chief of the armies, and sanctified by religious precedent. Today the beholder's inner eye must vividly clothe the imperial coinage with this potent philosophy, not very far removed from earthly worship, if his outer eye is to capture and enjoy its peculiar and characteristic beauties.

In other respects too Augustus made important changes in the appearance of the new imperial coinage. From now on, the coins were made in a relatively high relief, which tended to rise steadily and remained high for the next three hundred years. At no time, perhaps, was it ever so bold as that which had characterized some of the greater Greek masterpieces, but it was bold enough to encourage a genuinely plastic treatment of the portrait and to allow at least a plastic impressionism in the representation of full-length human figures and of animals. To some extent the size of imperial coins called for the heightening of relief to something like Hellenistic standards. For, while those of gold and silver for long continued to be comparatively small (smaller indeed than the standard size of Greek silver coins), those which were made of bright yellow brass and of ruddy copper were quite large, and went up to a full one and a half inches in diameter. Sometimes, indeed, this size was exceeded: the practice of producing medallions for presentation on special occasions became more frequent with the years, and these were often considerably larger (below, p. 92 f.). But in all these cases

71

there was an ample field available for the taste and ingenuity of the engravers, who turned it to fine advantage, the high relief combining with the natural beauty of the metal to produce an effect of gracefully robust exuberance. Lettering, too, now began to play its part. Its beauties of proportion, balance and discipline were a symptom of the Roman character at its best, and on these large coins it made a positive contribution, the influence of which has been felt ever since. By this the portraits were specially affected: henceforth they were framed by circular bands, or segments, of names and titles of elegant inscriptional form, strong enough to enclose yet seldom heavy enough to cramp the head accommodated, usually with such exquisite judgement, within. The finest coins of the Greeks had often shown a field occupied by a borderless, economical design of the greatest aesthetic integrity and power—the art (it will be remembered) of the seal-cutter, for whom no strong limitations exist. The coins of the Roman Empire, however, aimed at a different effect. Here the power was to come—and it came as a deliberate political suggestion—from everything that elaboration, fulness and balance could jointly contribute. At its worst the Roman idiom led to a fussy vulgarity or to confusion. But at its best it breathed the majestic plenitude of imperial power —complex, magnificently stable, yet always flexible.

The strength of the new idiom, in even its early stage of development under Augustus, is curiously illustrated by the morphology of the coins used in ancient Britain at this time. These, by an odd historical accident, were based in design upon the Greek coins made by Philip II of Macedon three hundred years earlier. Philip's designs—an elegant Apollo head (33), and a victorious charioteer—became well known in Gaul, whither his coins penetrated in quantity, for reasons still not certainly known, and there they were widely imitated. The rich, rounded head of Apollo was transmuted into a vast mass of formally curling hair, traversed by a gigantic wreath (34); beneath, the features of Apollo's face were preserved, in a scale not half that of the hair and wreath.

On the back the chariot, and all but a suggestion of the charioteer, disappeared; and the two horses were reduced to one. These coins in turn travelled to Britain, and in turn were imitated, from the middle of the first century B.C., by British artists who were at the peak of a Celtic florescence which delighted in all the interwoven curves and volutes seen, for example, in the Battersea shield at the British Museum. The eyes and the hands of these skilful men transmuted the often sprawling and unbalanced designs of Gaul into new and formal beauty. Apollo's features were abandoned: instead, British artists concentrated on the wreath, which was converted into a cross or curving whorl (35), elaborately decorated and inter-filled with annulets and crescents; and the horse on the back was rendered in a free schematic pattern familiar to those who have seen the White Horse carved on the Berkshire chalk downs at Uffington. Celtic art, it would seem, was constantly fluid: the coin-designs melt and fuse and re-form under our eyes from one kingdom to another, from one short span of years to the next, always in some process of adaptation or experiment. And we should have guessed that anything so spontaneously elegant was also naturally strong if it was not obvious that Roman art-forms, crossing the Channel peacefully in trade under Augustus (for the Roman conquest of Britain was still half a century away), had not within twenty years swept from the Celtic coinage all but the elementary traces of its former Celtic splendour, changing it—except in the far north— into something uncomfortably hybrid and increasingly ordinary. In particular it is plain that British artists were fascinated by Roman portrait-forms.

It was indeed on the portraits that the Roman die-engravers lavished their principal care and skill for some time to come. These portraits are of the utmost variety. Some are magnificent: nearly all are interesting, since from one reign to another they demonstrate the extent to which an emperor was willing to make art serve the cause of politics and able to call upon a supply of skilled artists. An emperor would normally wish to approve a basic likeness from which coin-portraits could subsequently be engraved. Much would naturally depend on the treatment shown in the approved model: this might be Hellenistic and "intense", or realistic in the later Republican tradition, or deliberately "old Roman"—hard and almost uncouth, and the differences would naturally be reflected in the coin-portraits which were based on such originals. Nevertheless, if ten men are set to copy a given original, it is very unlikely that ten identical copies will be produced. Each man will unconsciously allow his purely objective attention to be clouded momentarily, or diverted, by subjective feeling; and emphasis will vary as one man reads more into the eye, another into the mouth, and another into the proportions of the skull. As the Roman Empire grew older, means were evidently found of standardizing the concept of the imperial portrait in each reign, for variety becomes progressively less: perhaps the three-dimensional models officially distributed for imitation by the die-engravers were mass-produced by casting. Early in the Empire, however, the variety was great, and at no time more so than under Augustus.

He appears to have had many artists at his disposal, scattered through the numerous mints which he opened from time to time in Asia Minor, Rome, Gaul and Spain. Decentralization of minting must result in heterogeneous styles, and it is the fact that extreme variants of the Augustan portrait can be placed side by side and suggest the features of quite different men. But there is no doubt what Augustus wanted. With many Greek artists to call upon, especially in the east, he obviously favoured a portrait treatment in the Hellenistic rather than the Roman style, in which a certain impressionism in the rendering of the hair, an avoidance of any physical blemishes like lines or furrows, and a willingness to exaggerate the proportions of neck and forehead should produce an "ideal" likeness, helped by the most subtle and delicate technique. He was, wrote Suetonius, tall and graceful: rather careless in the dressing of his slightly curly auburn hair; and serene in expression. His eyes were bright and shining, and he was pleased if others felt that they exerted some dazzling, god-like compulsion—an effect increased by the shapeliness and proportion of his body, which somehow made him seem taller than others of his own height. One of his master-engravers brilliantly suggested these characteristics in a portrait (43) which must be counted as among the finest of the early Empire. The hair, thick and a little tousled, frames a face of serene strength, its passions contained and controlled but suggested, by the mere possession of gentle beauty, to an age which did not dissociate physical from intellectual excellence. The features are fine-drawn, slender and graceful: the eye looks widely forth, thoughtfully but without expressed emotion, exactly as in the many Greek coin-portraits of Apollo. And it was as the human counterpart of Apollo that Augustus conceived himself when he instituted special worship to Apollo, the young, strong, beautiful god whose majesty was seen no less in peace than in war. This portrait by an unknown master—its only aesthetic foil the simple inscription behind the head— presented the new lord of the earth in the finest Greek-derived idiom, assisted by all that first-class plastic skill could do.

But tradition and opportunity were to vary. With Claudius new influences were felt. In studied contrast to the despotism of Tiberius and Caligula he preached the doctrine that an emperor, however great, was no more than a man. His reign saw what was clearly an attempt to form a new imperial tradition in die-engraving, and calls attention to the extraordinary fluctuations in the style of coin-portraiture that took place at this period. Augustus, as we have seen, was portrayed by his most brilliant artists in a manner which, derived from the Hellenistic, subordinated realism to an idealizing treatment in which the spiritual qualities were eloquently expressed. Under Tiberius and Caligula artists were not concerned with the spiritual qualities of the emperors whose likenesses they made, nor even with those ethical characteristics which had contributed so much interest to Republican portraits of the realist school: instead they concentrated on the strong and often ruthless structural forms in the faces of those who ruled the world. With Claudius (45) the treatment changed again. Not only was the technical work of engraving carried out with far more delicacy and a far greater attention to the interplay of subtly modelled planes than had been seen since Augustus, but for the first time this skill in technique is combined with an ethical treatment of the features which results in much more than dry realism. If one had to decide at what time Roman imperial coin-portraiture first ascended to that height of skilful engraving, subjectively appreciated character, and fidelity neither idealizing nor dry, on which it was so long to remain the answer would almost certainly be that it happened under Claudius. His portraits stand before us grandly conceived, delicately expressed, showing just enough of realism in the representation of puckered brow, anxiously intent eye and constrained mouth to suggest the mood of purpose and perplexity in a man who sought to reconcile the tenets of Stoic philosophy with supreme personal power. This is an art in which the judicious selection of features for accurate representation produces a limited realism in which there is room besides for the purely subjective suggestion of intellectual and emotional qualities.

With Nero there was yet another change. An emperor who prided himself upon his aesthetic sense and talent, and for whom a prolonged visit to Greece was perhaps the major event in a life of artistic frustration, would scarcely leave to chance the engraving of his portrait dies, especially as he took the trouble to introduce elaborate and far-reaching reforms in his whole coinage-system. His portraits (46) show a recession from the "idealized mood" seen under Claudius to something less personal and more generalized. No engraver could fail to represent the thick flesh, lowering eyes, and small hard mouth riding arrogantly above the jutting chin and fat jowl. But these features were treated as basic essentials

EARLY ROMAN IMPERIAL PORTRAITURE

$\dfrac{45}{\dfrac{46}{47}}$ 45 Claudius (p. 75 f.), 46 Nero (p. 76 f.), 47 Galba (p. 81)

EARLY ROMAN IMPERIAL DESIGN

48, 49 Tiberius (p. 84 f.), 50 Galba (p. 86 f.)

of form and contour, and not so much as an index of character, eloquent though they might be. The power of the Neronian portrait came rather from the baroque grandeur of its whole conception—the great head, often tilted slightly upwards upon the heavy column of the neck, its thick and curling hair elaborately dressed above the forehead. This is the dramatic magnificence of a demi-god or hero; and the appropriate vehicle for such a representation was the heroic idealism of the Hellenistic school, with its studious avoidance of detail, its love of full, rounded forms and its patent enjoyment of decorative adjuncts.

A century and a half had passed since the first true portraits appeared on Roman coinage. At first they had been tentative, their undoubted power being lessened by a tradition of inferior technique. But the increasing infusion of Greek artists and of Greek standards of engraving, combined with the cool, characteristically Roman ability of observing human physiognomy and deducing inner character, swiftly built up a mastery in coin-portraiture. This mastery long continued to be the special excellence of Roman coinage, and its influence was to affect all European die-engravers, in varying degree, down to the present day.

CHAPTER V

Art and Politics under the Roman Empire

NERO'S death in A.D. 68 extinguished the Blessed Augustus' line. When Julius Caesar had been murdered, over a century before, and Augustus had rebuilt the structure of the state, there had been no general sense of the end of one epoch and the beginning of the next. But the death of Nero closed an epoch so clearly that few could fail to understand it. The imperial system of government had come to stay: the question at issue was simply how to fill the vacuum caused by the disappearance of the last of the Augustan dynasty.

In a single year four claimants contested for imperial power until Vespasian, the fourth, triumphed. All four struck coins, and these show that, from the point of view of imperial portraiture, the result would have been the same whoever had emerged successful. The curiously brilliant blend of political idealism and human realism which the portraits of Claudius had suddenly developed was now revived again as the standard method of representing the temporal holder of what was almost divinely wide power. If anything, the element of realism was increased, for the relief of coins in general was heightened, and with this higher relief the die-engravers found new opportunities for plastic skill in the rendering of planes, so that eyes could be deeper set, furrows more strongly marked, and the general interplay of light and shade much more dramatically arranged. But, although realism was thus intensified, the sense of political idealism was by no means neglected. The emperors were deliberately marked as the occupants of an exalted office, which should continue as long as Rome should continue, by various adjuncts carefully selected so as to frame the man within the setting of the office. The laurel wreath usually sits upon the imperial brow, and to this are added such extra touches as armour and drapery; the effect, accordingly, is that of a portrait rendered in a highly individual and realistic style but, so to speak, wearing the insignia of an office which claimed his duty and his labour on behalf of a world-wide empire. This was political portraiture at its very highest.

Thus we see Galba (47) the first of the claimants for Nero's position. The large, strong, square head—harsher, indeed, than the idiom of imperial coinage had previously favoured—fills most of the field left vacant by the band of bold and clear lettering. The old man's features are shown with combined magnificence and fidelity: fidelity, because of the care taken with the stern eye and grimly set mouth and heavy furrows; magnificence, because the sense of scale and proportion, together with the armour and imperial aegis, mark this old man out as the gifted holder of immense and exceptional power. With Vespasian, the victorious *bourgeois*, the sense of realism is temporarily increased at the expense of political idealism: the wreath sits upon a great, inelegant head so closely cropped as to lack all subtlety of line, and the coarse folds of the throat and the nape of the neck are echoed by those of a fleshy forehead frowning intently above a short and thickened nose. His sons and successors, first Titus, and then Domitian, moved away from this almost earthy quality of Vespasian's realism. Furrows were diminished: the hair was shown in a careful arrangement of longer, artless locks; and the fleshy contours, which the artist's hand has not allowed time to harrow or to ravage, speak of that abundant virility, that distinctive well-being, neither soft nor feminine, which was noted in the idealizing portraits of Greek gods, heroes and nymphs in the fifth and fourth centuries. With Trajan, again, a new school of portrait-artists was at work. Relief became lower, the forms were flatter and harder, and the accompanying lettering shrank

81

in size: for two decades a sense of sterility and restriction pervaded the increasingly abundant coinage of the Roman mint.

Within a century and a half of the collapse of the Roman Republic, therefore, imperial portraiture had developed a technical skill which rivalled that of any earlier age of die-engravers and a conceptual quality, politically idealist and personally realist, which set it apart from any earlier idiom. The imperial achievement in respect of non-portrait designs was far less remarkable. Whereas on Greek coins the normal foil to the obverse head of god or nymph or king had been a reverse design of clear and simple national symbolism, calling for little change except in the progressive spirit and manner of its treatment, Roman coins from quite early times were required to show reverses which told a story, proclaimed new fact, or pointed a moral. And after the Augustan Empire was established this tendency was strengthened: while the obverse portrait displayed the emperor of the day the reverse design called attention to some aspect of his achievement or policy—in a manner and with a constantly varying aptitude which (as has now been abundantly proved) points to the operation of official choice. Throughout the ages the designers of coins have had to take orders in regard to their designs. But the limitations have varied widely. Greek artists, required to represent a simple national symbol, could exercise their judgement in making it more or less decorative and elaborate. The artists of medieval Europe, as we shall similarly see, if they were ordered to show a monarch on his throne or on horseback, could treat this central theme in whatever manner their instinct suggested so long as the theme was in fact reproduced. But when an artist was told "Show the emperor, the Roman-clad symbol of Rome, receiving from a kneeling Parthian, in Parthian dress, one of the veritable standards captured from the unlucky Crassus" or "Show the Goddess of the imperial corn-supply receiving the corn-ships which have docked safely in Italy," or (to take an example from narrower imperial symbolism) "Show the goddess of Fair-dealing personified, holding her appropriate scales and horn of plenty," the factual element of the Roman character was imposing limitations upon die-engravers which even the best and most inventive artist could not evade.

The strength of these official influences can be judged well by a glance at the subject-matter of gems carved in the imperial epoch. These often show portrait heads, of course; but, where they do not, they delight in the representation either of mythological scenes and creatures, or of beasts and birds, or of the human figure conceived in the most sculptural possible idiom. They had no special story to transmit: their designs might indeed be specially suggested or commissioned, but in treatment they reflected the free taste and the balanced judgement of the artists themselves. By contrast the reverse designs of the imperial coinage present us with many examples of most disappointing quality. Coins which are ennobled by a splendid obverse portrait may be demeaned by a reverse which is poor both in conception and execution. It was one thing to make a portrait, infused with all that the artist's eye and the prevailing political climate could contribute: in this his hand would work its fullest skill. It was quite another thing to engrave some stock symbol, some personification of imperial virtue so lacking in character that special adjuncts were necessary for identification, or to devise some multi-figure scene which would fit only with great difficulty into a coin's circular field.

Such were the problems which faced the engravers at this period, and it is a credit to their ingenuity and essential artistry that they did in fact produce so many reverse designs which, in one way or another, are outstandingly successful. A number of the best were undoubtedly adapted from sculptural groups by artists who showed their skill not least in transmuting a solid three-dimensional design, standing free in space, into a miniature low-relief design bounded by a firm circumference. Among such artists was the nameless master who engraved the superlative portrait of Augustus described above (p. 75). His portrait was accompanied by a reverse (44) of the highest Graeco-Roman quality. The cow (or heifer, or steer?) may conceivably have had some politically symbolist aptitude, though this must be conjectural: what is certain is that the artist conceived and contrived a design of that same integrated simplicity that distinguished the Greek masters. Its relief, of course, is lower than that of the Greek masterpieces of an earlier age, but thereby the artist's problems were increased, for he was compelled to work in the most subtle of planes in order to achieve his effect of sleek and muscular strength. His model, as need not be doubted, was one of those bronze beasts which even today grace the squares and market-places of Mediterranean lands. A second example of design borrowed and adapted from monumental sculpture is furnished by the Victory reverses on Vespasian's coins. Here, in a larger field, the whole composition is itself larger, and foreshadows the magnificent medallions of the time of Hadrian and Antoninus Pius: the relief is high, and, although the execution is considerably less delicate than in the Augustan die, the general effect of robust and decorative splendour—the essence of the Graeco-Roman sculptured original as it must have been—is admirably suggested.

Just occasionally an artist was found in this earlier period who was prepared to experiment with design of a more formal kind. Thus, when twin sons were born to Drusus, the son of Tiberius, opportunity was brilliantly seized (48). The motif of crossed horns of plenty was not new to the Roman coinage, and in itself it proved to be a pattern and a composition of obvious attractiveness within the circular field of a coin. The charm of the Tiberian composition, however, lay in the combination of various factors—the babies' heads placed, all unselfconscious, upon the crossed horns: the vertical caduceus centrally placed, light and graceful, yet strong enough to give balance and height to the design; and, above all, the absence of all lettering at a time when lettering was, on the whole, so well loved as a container, or at least an accessory, for almost any composition. This Tiberian conception stands out from among five centuries of Roman imperial coinage for its elegant formalism and its inner tenderness. It was, in fact, an obverse design, and the accompanying reverse (49) shows at once the versatility of Roman coin-artists and a fresh proof of their excellence in formal decoration. For it consists entirely of lettering. The centre is held by the large and gracefully formed capital letters S C (= Senatus Consulto, by decree of the Senate); and around the edge run the names and titles of Drusus himself, in whose name Tiberius coined this complimentary piece. Design created purely out of lettering is most difficult to achieve successfully: all too easily it may assume the appearance of a portion punched out of a larger page or document. But it is justified if the layout is subtly balanced—as it is here by smaller letters revolving in a band around larger, "fixed" ones—and if the letter-forms themselves are well enough proportioned; and here those forms are exquisitely slim and delicate.

In their attempt to get away from the mass of stereotyped conceptions which imperial policy forced upon them, the Roman coin-designers produced many architectural compositions, showing temples and public buildings, and under Nero went so far as to create an aerial view of the fine new harbour at Ostia, its arms safely enclosing a number of ships riding quietly at anchor with their sails furled. But all such experiments are more interesting, or more curious, than they are beautiful. The Greek masters had clearly shown that the essence of successful coin-design was the sudden immobilization, for a given moment of observation on the small area of a coin, of forms which in life are fluent with motion or colour or both: hardly ever did they attempt to render a widely set scene in the pictorial manner employed in so many modern postage-stamps, with their buildings and townscapes and harbours. It may be assumed that the best Roman die-engravers, nurtured in the Greek tradition, agreed with the earlier masters, for although it is true that many coins locally produced in the Greek east under Roman rule do in fact present elaborately pictorial scenes, often in considerable three-dimensional depth like modern stamps, it is also true that such coins were deliberately designed to play the part of such stamps, advertising local buildings and shrines as widely as possible in regions expected to preserve a sense of their antiquarian or tourist interest. For the central imperial coinage these considerations scarcely applied: here the designs, as we have seen, were intended to serve broad imperial motives of political expediency and not those of local pride.

There was, however, one further basic design which the Roman coin-artists developed to a high level of excellence—the multi-figure group usually showing the emperor addressing soldiers or citizens. It is likely that this motif was borrowed from sculptured originals: not, however, in this case from sculpture in the round but rather from reliefs. If so their achievement was all the greater. A frieze is a continuous ribbon of alternating rest and movement. To isolate a segment in so economical a way that it does not spill over the natural limits (as happens, for example, in Italian maiolica ware), and yet to preserve its closely knit significance, is a task so difficult that few artists attempted it and fewer still succeeded. The first serious essay was made in the time of Caligula, whose artists showed him, mounted on a platform, addressing a token group of five soldiers, all uniformly smaller than the stature of the emperor himself. Just as the portraits of Caligula were hard and insensitive, so also was this reverse design, composed of uncompromising verticals, the one larger and taller than the others. Further experiment was made under Nero, the component figures being more loosely grouped; but here flexibility was achieved at the cost of integrity, the composition breaking up to the extent of suggesting that some excerpt from a larger design had been arbitrarily enclosed within the coin's circular shape. True mastery over the multi-figure subject was achieved only under Galba, a calm appraisal of whose coins strongly suggests that, however ephemeral his reign and however uncompromising his personal characteristics, the collapse of the Neronian régime liberated powerful forces among the coin-designers

STYLE UNDER HADRIAN AND ANTONINUS

51, 52 Hadrian (p. 91 f.), 53, 54 Antoninus (p. 96 f.)

55
—
56
—
57

ROME: RETURN FROM IDEALISM TO REALISM

55, 56 Commodus (p. 97), 57 Caracalla (p. 98)

of the day. In contrast to the design which had shown Caligula addressing a knot of soldiers, Galba's version of the same subject (50) represented profound advance. It is the property of a frieze to express a message in a kind of rhythm, long subjects alternating with shorter ones, violence with repose. Whereas the artists of Caligula and Nero had been unable to abbreviate this sense of rhythm within the compass of a coin, those of Galba were markedly successful: they suggested depth, and variation in height was aptly used to avoid the monotony of earlier designs. This masterly coin expresses the whole magnificent essence of the early Empire—strong and crowded, its natural turbulence disciplined by a knowledge of the imperial ideal.

With Galba, indeed, the artistry of the Roman imperial coinage had reached a new height and a new triumph. The portraits, as we have seen earlier, combined realism with a truly imperial splendour; and the reverse designs—larger, bolder and sculpturally more sensitive and discriminating than anything which had preceded them—enable us to postulate a new school of die-engravers with a new artistic vision. These characteristics continued, with slow decline, during the Flavian dynasty of Vespasian, Titus and Domitian. Their coin-portraiture was normally fine, but increasingly lost its inner strength; and the reverses, often splendid, showed a steady loss of those qualities of experiment and vision which had so dramatically marked the short reign of Galba. This was a generation in which die-engravers followed —and worked out—a new idiom; and its ultimate poverty can be observed in the slipshod workmanship of Nerva's coins. With Trajan some attempt was made to substitute something better, but evidently the artists were lacking. Trajanic art-forms, so far as coinage was concerned, were hard and narrow. Relief was flattened: lettering became small and almost mean; and the treatment of the human form was little more than perfunctory. Nevertheless, the reign of Trajan turned the first leaf in the golden chapter of peace and culture which was to make famous the years of Hadrian

and Antoninus Pius: in particular it presented to the world
the conception of an emperor selected and admired because
he possessed, in his own character and not from any accident
of birth or lineage, the qualities of a noble, just, strong and
successful ruler. At the end of Trajan's reign there was at
least one first-class die-engraver, known from a single surviving coin, whose work makes it certain that the flowering
of the engraver's art under Hadrian was not due simply to
Hadrian's own artistic policy as emperor; for this Trajanic
artist was undoubtedly the partial author of artistic traditions
which are to be seen and enjoyed under Hadrian.

But it is true that Hadrian's personal influence on the feeling and idiom of imperial art—in coinage no less than in other
forms of expression—was intensely strong. Nor was this
unnatural under an emperor who himself possessed an expert
knowledge of painting, found his favourite architect in
Apollodorus of Damascus, spoke Greek and Latin with equal
proficiency, modelled his appearance (with the short Greek
beard) upon classical Greek lines, and even tried his own
hand—amid a life of ceaseless business and travel—at
sculpture and painting. But the change marked by Hadrianic
art, so far as it affected his coin-designers, was no mere
reversion to "classical" idealism or revival of "classical"
forms. Conscious restoration of past idioms is seldom achieved
without an obvious sacrifice of feeling, so clear, for example,
in the nineteenth-century classical revival. It is not enough
to repeat the forms with full mathematical exactitude, for the
feeling which originally infused those forms when they first
appeared, compounded as it was of everything which contemporary manners and traditions could contribute, is something that no later age can counterfeit in perfection—a lesson
which many forgers, in their own way, come to recognize.
The classical revival under Hadrian was something of another
kind. It is to be seen in the employment of much more
delicate execution than the imperial coinage had ever before
received, and in equally delicate conception. It is as if his
coin-designers were schooled, deeply and quite suddenly, in

the comparative appreciation of the best art-forms of previous epochs, thus gaining a more subtle vision and a more sensitive hand. Their work could easily have become academic, or, at the best, eclectic; and it is true that many of the lesser engravers failed conspicuously in a period of new ideals. But these very ideals were the cause, with the greater Hadrianic engravers, of a new strength and splendour. For these men were concerned with the representation, in the forms of classical idealism, of the personality of an emperor who, unlike his predecessors, was neither dynast nor conqueror, being emperor rather because he showed a noble combination of all noble virtues. Idealism, if its object is positive and deeply felt, can seldom become stale or academic. The best Hadrianic engravers were artists whose technical skill was matched by equally deep feeling, and their work shines, among much that is ordinarily competent, with all the polish of a gem and the easy perfection of a masterpiece. They should have been allowed or encouraged to leave us their names.

Like other engravers of the preceding half-century and more, these Hadrianic artists preferred to work within the ampler limits of the larger dies which bronze coinage and medallions called for. In particular, they were able thereby to design portraits of extraordinary grandeur and delicacy. Two, of strongly contrasted treatment, may be compared. The first is that on a large brass coin, and shows the head and neck only (51). The proportions are generous: the large head, with its broad, flat crown, its full and bearded cheek and sturdy neck, impress the eye with the suggestion of proportional size not hitherto seen on the imperial coinage. But the artist has also known how to play with space—that supreme test of a die-engraver, and has skilfully isolated the emperor's image in a solitary splendour. This splendour, however, owes nothing to studied elaboration. Hadrian wears no wreath; and there is no imperial drapery from which the conception can gain potency. The emperor is acting no part save that of Hadrian himself; his features are rendered in the softest strength by a skill which gives shadow to his thoughtful, steady eye, and the sole decoration comes from what is truly decorative, namely, the fine and gentle waves of the luxuriant hair and beard. High artistry and exquisitely sensitive taste succeed in concentrating the observer's total attention upon the emperor's qualities of spirit and intellect.

The second portrait is fashioned in a different idiom. It shows Hadrian's figure, in the strictest profile, down to his upper arm and breast (52). The treatment is unusually statuesque, and the artist—surely that same man who experimented with just such another portrait for Trajan—has developed so masterly a technique in the engraving of different planes that the resultant play of light and shade suggests the relief of a deeply carved frieze in stone. Hadrian's head, now wreathed, rises to the top of the circular field, and all but pierces the dotted border: the arm and the breast—heavy, yet sleek and strong—extend to the very bottom. The strength of this full-chested, pyramidal design is accentuated by the imperial cloak which, clasped on the emperor's shoulder, falls in a lovely curve which frames his arm behind and cascades in folds over his breast in front. But the designer of this majestic portrait—nearly half-length, and splendid in imperial vestment—has not relied upon these unaccustomed elements for the suggestion of Hadrian's personality. Serene strength and grace of feature are again presented to us, with no less delicacy than in the first portrait: the only difference is that in this half-length portrait Hadrian is shown in an essentially imperial guise. The distinction is one well known and understood by people content to invest their monarchs with the outward symbols of the grace, strength and beauty which exalted position is felt to demand. In one mood we delight in the symbols, and feel their deep powers of emotional suggestion. In another we prefer to remove them, and to reflect on the individual and personal qualities which are the justification of high and almost divine office.

Whereas the first of these two portraits appeared on an ordinary coin, produced for currency, the second and more elaborate one was made for a medallion. And the increased production of medallions under Hadrian—pieces specially designed, like so many later medals, for special presentation, and usually in a large size—gave to the artists of the day opportunities which had to a great extent been denied to their predecessors. For these pieces, not being intended for currency, were struck in small numbers; and limited production allowed the engravers to experiment with designs which, if they had been used for ordinary "currency" pieces, would have resulted in an unduly fast consumption of dies which plainly must have taken more than the normal time to create. As a result the subject-matter of medallions, both now and in succeeding reigns, differed from that of coins. The imperial portrait became more elaborately beautiful, and the reverses presented scenes likely to appeal to the more cultured and educated taste of those who were singled out to be recipients of medallions. Hadrian's passionate interest in classical Greek motifs consequently resulted in their frequent adoption by his leading die-engravers for the reverses of medallions.

But these artists did not merely revive Greek idiom or rethink Greek ideas. They might indeed borrow liberally from the visual vocabulary of Greek myth and legend, moving away—as medallions allowed them to move away— from the conventional political conceptions on the reverses of coins proper. Nevertheless they went much further than this. the conventional conceptions, by an almost incessant process of repetition, had become sterile in form because they were so often sterile in feeling—stock figures conveying a stock message, and did not encourage artists, still less oblige them, to try new formulae of composition. By contrast the renewal of interest in the subject-matter of Greek art furnished them with a galaxy of forms, situations and emotions which until now no die-engraver had ever attempted to compose and express. In the quality of their reactions the artists varied considerably. Some merely took the opportunity afforded by a large-sized coin in high relief, often without a reverse-inscription, to give a bolder and more robust treatment, rendered with much greater plastic feeling, to more or less

93

conventional figures and compositions. Others, however—
and we should give much to learn the names of those few
master-engravers who must have influenced them—developed
an entirely new formula in feeling and composition. Whereas
previous Roman coin-design had been fundamentally still in
feeling (as still, indeed, as the powerful forms of the imperial
portrait, however much instinct with personality), they now
desired and secured movement, almost as if seeking to
re-create the remarkable sense of motion which so many
Greek coins normally expressed. And whereas previously the
Roman engravers had avoided any hint of romantic treatment, master-artists now experimented with a simple but
brilliant symbolism which seemed to set the human figure
against a formal landscape in which human emotion and
human action could be more passionately suggested. Finally,
as was natural in a school which drew its inspiration from
classical Greek traditions, the human figure was now often
represented nude, so that full advantage could be taken (as
the Greeks before had taken it) of bodily forms as the
expression of personality.

A simple example of the new idiom, made under Hadrian,
is to be seen and enjoyed on the reverse of a small and delightful medallion of bronze. The goddess Salus stands by the
altar reserved for sacrifices to her. She is naked except for a
light fold of drapery, drawn in such a way across her thighs
that the rounded complexity of Praxitelean forms is emphasized: her hips are full, her legs crossed in the elegant leisure
of an idle, private moment. Perhaps not quite idle, however,
for her hand is extended across the altar to feed the sacred
serpent whose home it was. And the serpent, which in the
plainer idiom of ordinary coins rises always from the altar
itself, is here no small or undecorative creature. Coil upon
coil it has climbed up the trunk of a small tree, and, its upper
part safely balanced in the branches, stretches out its head
to accept the offering which the goddess makes. In this soft,
sinuous and artfully balanced composition there is nothing to
disturb the deep harmony of form or feeling. No circular

inscription distracts the eye: the only lettering (and this, as taste grew, would certainly be omitted) consisted of the goddess's name in small characters upon her garlanded altar. This reverse was a work of art, made in a small scale, but well pondered. The engraver resisted the temptation to place the design centrally in the field available to him: if he had done so the mass of the human body, heavy in relation to the slight forms of tree and writhing serpent, would have been cramped by the border. As a result he produced a design of which the deliberate unbalance, the curving forms, the dramatic suggestion of motion in the serpent's attitude, and the tree with its symbolical suggestion of a world of reality as the setting for a goddess whom no man saw, combine in a conception of great distinction and beauty.

With Antoninus Pius the new idioms were powerfully developed, and compositions acquired a broad pictorial quality and often became astonishingly elaborate in detail. The artists who conceived these Antonine designs were men whose eye was, indeed, safely fixed on the classical motifs and models of the past. But their feeling, so far from being that which infused classical Greek design, is purely Roman; and, in its attention to detail, its love of complex balance (reflected also in the oratory of this Silver Age), and its romantic appreciation of the natural elements in the physical scene around them, it looked curiously forward, spanning a thousand years and more, and offered itself as the quintessence of what Renaissance artists came to love so deeply. Two bronze Antonine medallions show the full flowering of the art. On the first Mercury—nude except for a light cloak hanging from his shoulders—walks delicately, springily towards a garlanded pillar. With his right arm he leads a prancing ram: the caduceus held in the crook of his left arm provides an easy, natural balance for the gesture of the right arm. Behind, a gnarled and leafless tree curves past him and above his head, as successful in its directional emphasis as it is in providing a foil to the finely rendered muscular form of the young god. The second (54) is a stylized landscape. To the

95

left a bridge rears its great bulk, vividly suggested by its foreshortened forms. Through it a galley forces its way, its bows cleaving a turbulent stream in which sits the welcoming Tiber god himself. From the bows of the vessel a serpent, closely coiled, stretches its head to a rocky shore where stand a tree and temples. In this astonishing composition, which fills the whole field and yet does not cram it, we see again the contemporary fondness for fluid serpentine forms and for the delicate balance of trees. The serpent, indeed, binds the whole design together with an instantaneous (almost electric) intensity, and enabled the artist to produce a design in which many different elements—animate and inanimate forms, perspective, height, distance, solid and fluid matter— are dramatically combined.

If a seemingly disproportionate amount of space has here been given to the school of engravers which grew up under Hadrian's care and flourished freely under Antoninus it is because it marks one of those great steps forward, in the direction of new feeling and experimental design, on which depends the continued health and vigour of any such phy- sically limited art as that of coinage. In the Roman coinage the conception of living portraiture had been the first great step: the ennobling of living portraiture into something that was part-individualistic but also part-idealistic was the second. And now, for a period of three-quarters of a century, there was added the new element—the ability to turn reverse- design, primarily on medallions but also, through their influence, on ordinary coins as well, into new channels of free and elaborate composition in which was needed the same skill demanded by the finest of portraits. Under Marcus Aurelius and Commodus the new tradition continued, and artists created a series of exquisitely conceived and admirably engraved dies. There were signs, perhaps, that the new impulses were slowly working themselves out. Reverse- designs tended to lose a little of their delicacy of treatment and discreet balance. The distinction, always previously valid, between the first-class work of the medallion-artist and the lower quality of the coin-dies became more strongly marked. Moreover, the artists appear to have lost something of that excellence in the plastic rendering of their dies which had made the high relief of Hadrian's pieces at once so magnificent and so sensitive. The sensitive element now slowly diminished: that of magnificence increased, until the Severan dynasty at the beginning of the third century initiated yet another tradition.

Nevertheless, the dying years of the second century produced much work of memorable beauty. The portraits of Antoninus (53) had breathed a sweet gravity which the shadowed careful eye, set above a long thin nose, acquitted always of serene complacency and to which a gently fluid mobility was imparted by the delicate treatment of hair and beard. Under Commodus, as the forms became gradually harder, the purely decorative element increased, until the little boy whose plump and happy portrait had appeared, with that of the young Annius Verus, on a little medallion of unforced charm and almost Renaissance directness, was presented in all the elaborate magnificence of highly charged classical idiom. A superb medallion (55) shows him as the incarnate Hercules he claimed to be, his head covered with the hero's Lion-skin, his eyes heavy and shadowed as they looked ponderingly out upon the range of his human labours. The reverse (56) completes the imagery of the imperial hero. Wreathed for victory he stands, by a sculptor's conceit, turned away from the beholder: the muscles of his naked back and legs are deeply shadowed, and the knees are gently bent in momentary relaxation as he gazes sideways at the Nemean lion lying dead upon a rock before him. The splendour and boldness of the artist's concept are unmistakable; but his technique, compared with the best work under Hadrian and Antoninus, already shows a loss of delicacy.

The output of medallions sharply diminished after the death of Commodus, and it was on the ordinary coinage of Severus and his son Caracalla that the art of the engraver was principally to be seen. Dies mass-produced could never match the polished perfection of those made specially for medallions: nevertheless, the standard of Severan portraiture was high. These emperors and their successors were for the most part military autocrats, thrown up from this province or from that, by an incessant process of turmoil or usurpation, to assume supreme power at Rome. The highly civilized, peaceful and paternalistic principles of government which Hadrian and the Antonines had formulated were swept away by the savage necessities of imperial rivalry and imperial defence. Accordingly the portrait-tradition changed, and we see the emperors presented with a ruthless fidelity curiously devoid of humane content—strong, hard men like Caracalla himself (57), with foreheads wrinkled and heavily furrowed above stern eyes which seem to watch their empire with unblinking suspicion. Indeed it was as if the portraiture of the age of Galba and Vespasian—a century and a half before— had been taken up again and developed logically from the point at which the Hadrianic school of artists had ousted it; and the impression of deliberate resumption is strengthened by the reverse designs of Severus and his successors, which lose the touch of fluency and poetry and busy themselves again with purely conventional subjects conventionally (and uncritically) rendered.

But the artistry of Roman coinage, which ultimately drew its strength at all times from the strength of the political philosophy underlying the imperial system itself, was not yet to degenerate by ceaseless repetition of stereotyped subjects: the engravers of a new age were still to develop new conceptions and new styles under the stimulus of new political theory. Already, the near-collapse of the Roman Empire under Gallienus in the middle of the third century revealed new impulses in style and fresh values in portraiture. Gallienus himself, high-born and sophisticated, attempted to foster a re-birth of the "classical" glories of Hadrianic and Antonine art, and his portraits, which began in the harder style prevalent since Severus, softened into the considered balance and delicacy of an earlier, richer and more peaceful age, showing him in a very strongly idealistic idiom. His small elegant head was gently rendered in a relief much lower than was usually normal before, and the engravers suggested the emperor's personality not by rigid attention to the individualism of his features but by the air of general grace which he wore—seen, for example, in the frequent upward tilt given to the head in conformity with Hellenistic practice since the days of Alexander the Great.

A different idiom sprang up and flourished momentarily in Gaul, which seceded for half a generation under emperors of its own. In contrast to the fluctuating tradition among the engravers in the capital, now realist, now idealist, but always possessed of a fine sophistication and economy—sometimes even to the point of sterility, the Gallic artists were of a robust and lively school, delighting in all the profusion of rounded forms and loosely curling hair which the polite school of Rome had for long avoided. Moreover, they were ready to attempt what no skilled engraver had attempted for centuries on the dies for a mass-produced coinage, namely, a nearly facing portrait (58); and, in attempting this, they achieved what the Greek master-engravers also had achieved—the sudden, startling sense of intimacy between the viewer and the image viewed. Postumus, emperor in Gaul, faces us in full provincial strength and ebullience, qualities not inappropriate to that Hercules whom he particularly revered but with whom he never claimed personal identity, like Commodus. His features are full, almost rotund, and framed by the waving locks of thick bushy hair and luxuriant beard: the eyes are large, and the lips generous and voluptuous. This is a portrait in which the rounded planes of high relief reflect the light in an extraordinarily lively manner.

But it was not from the revived classicism of Gallienus nor from the new and healthy vigour of Postumus' artists that the ultimately dominant influences were to arise. Already, for a long time, the empire's military centre of gravity had been shifting eastward from the Rhine to the Balkan provinces adjoining the Danube, and the time was soon to come when, out of four joint imperial colleagues, not one made his capital at Rome, and when Constantine the Great founded his New Rome at Constantinople. From the east, therefore, were drawn new styles and idioms, in which a formal symbolism was the prevalent feature, matching the change which took place in the imperial status itself when, with political and military stability restored by super-administrators like Diocletian and Constantine, the head of the empire could again be viewed as a man of more than human greatness. In the mints of the west, of course, the old tradition of realism still remained, though even a Gallic mint could quickly show the austere tinge of the new formality, as in the Trèves gold medallion (59) with the portrait of Constantius, one of Diocletian's junior partners. Here the artist has observed realism in the general shape of head and features, and in the elaboration of drapery and armour on shoulders and breast; but the hair and beard, close cropped, have not been allowed to serve as a means of expression: the eye, little shadowed, does not so much ponder as scan objectively; and the forehead wears the furrows of all foreheads. In the east, however, the stylistic revolution was complete and at once showed extraordinary power. A gold medallion from the mint of Asiatic Nicomedia presents Diocletian in the new idiom (61). The portrait is entirely unadorned by any adjunct, however simple. That it represents Diocletian and not one of his three partners is made plain by the shape of his nose and—possibly— of his eyebrow. But in all other respects this is a symbolical representation. It is certainly not idealist, since idealism in portraiture seeks to express the highest human qualities, universally respected, by subordinating the force of individual characteristics. And here those characteristics are vividly suggested—the wide, open eye; the triple-furrowed brow; the small, set mouth. But they are not represented realistically: by yet a new twist in idiom the artist has universalized what earlier artists had always individualized, emperor by emperor. These are the eye and the mouth and the furrowed brow of all emperors whatsoever. The potency of

100

ROME: NEW STYLES OF THE LATER EMPIRE.

LATE ROMAN CEREMONIAL PORTRAITURE

62, 63 Constantine (p. 103), 64 Constantius II (p. 104)

the new style is thus drawn from its very character of symbolism.

A generation later the process had developed still further. Long before his formal conversion to Christianity Constantine had associated himself with Christian policy, and his finer portraits show the upward-tilted head of the man with his mind on the heavens (62), or the facing head, dazzling within its halo, of the world's half-Christian master (63). The two strands of tradition visible in Diocletian's time are still visible in Constantine's, the facing head preserving the decorative semi-realism of the medallion of Constantius, the tilted profile carrying on the stern, pure symbolism of Diocletian's. But in both these Constantinian portraits there is an access of formality—almost of hieratic power and grace. In the tilted profile, only the profile itself declares the portrait to be Constantine's: for the rest, no personal peculiarities, no coarsenesses of lineament, no slightest furrow or frown, are allowed to influence the symbolical image, the aesthetic beauty of which lies in the contrast between the flat, even relief of the face and neck and the exquisite engraving of the hair beneath its jewelled diadem. The facing head, as always, establishes a direct emotional reaction with the viewer; but the emotion is that proper to the observation of a ceremonial figure—part soldier, part priest, part lawyer, part administrator—in whose care were placed the destinies of the world; and the decorative adjuncts are purely subjective in their appeal.

As the fourth century passed the symbolist idiom became more and more strongly marked. The imperial portrait, still flatter in relief, and with the proportions of the head ever taller and thinner, is devoid of all expressed emotion whatever. By a curious turn of the wheel its effect on the beholder is not unlike that of the early heads of gods on Greek coins: there is the same sense of inward power, the same suggestion of combined remoteness and presence—the remoteness due to the utterly dispassionate treatment, the presence affirmed by the widely open eye which, equally curiously, in its own turn loses something of its previously standard profile treatment and begins to present a "primitive" frontal aspect again. Under Constantius II, in particular, the engravers of the mid-fourth century reached a noble level in this art of remote and almost priestly representation (64). Sometimes the emperor's hand might be raised in the attitude of benediction: more often the portrait derived its power from the mere suggestion of majesty undisturbed.

In the reverse designs of the fourth century the general standard of conception and execution was much lower. As a rule, the finest were reserved for the largest coins and for medallions, and in these we can see how artists attempted, from time to time, to escape from conventional subjects and conventional arrangement. The artist who designed the great medallion of Constantius, already noted (p. 100), still clung to the realist tradition in representation and sought, by a variation of levels which is more curious than beautiful, to landscape the whole dramatic scene of Constantius' arrival in the Thames and his welcome by the city of London (60). For the rest, emperors gallop into the fray, or stand fast holding the Christian banner, or are crowned by angels of victory, or drag unresisting and miniature prisoners into Roman captivity, or make elaborate ceremonies of sacrifice; and in all such standard subjects the artistry is perfunctory and negligible. But in the end symbolism affected the reverses too, and enabled designers to amplify the spirit of the portrait, as when the emperor sits formally enthroned in his imperial robes, holding sceptre and victory on orb, or rides in almost holy state in his ornate carriage with its six horses parted three this way and three that, so as to display the venerated central figure, his hand raised in blessing. Such symbolism, strong enough to survive imperial collapse in the fifth century and the age of darkness afterwards, was a most powerful influence on later civilizations. The status of the emperor was changing into that of King by the grace of God.

CHAPTER VI

Medieval and Byzantine Formalism

IT is very easy, in the automatic expectation of the many centuries of splendid European culture that were to come, to pass quickly over the four or five hundred years that followed the weakening of the Roman Empire in the west in the late fourth century. Yet for the western provinces of that Empire in particular the Roman collapse was a sombre and then a terrible event. The whole complex economic structure, the familiar ways of life, even the familiar ways of thinking, were profoundly changed by the bursting of the imperial frontiers, which let in horde upon horde of "barbarian" (because unromanized) fighting peoples, nomadic and loosely knit but firm in allegiance to their kings. From the steppes of Asia came the Huns, piercing the Carpathian barrier in the early fifth century, and thereafter roaming central Europe under Attila. From north and east swept the Goths and Visigoths and Ostrogoths, forcing their way across Dniester and Danube into Greece, pouring thence through the length and breadth of Italy, piercing into southern Gaul. From the north again came the Vandals, whose astonishing wanderings led them at first backwards and forwards in central Europe and thence, plunging south, through Gaul and Spain and across the straits of Gibraltar into the heart of Roman Africa. Their paths, upon the map, present a fantastic network of twists and turns and intersections from which one fact is abundantly clear: the Roman Empire of the west, richly established upon the encircling ring of Mediterranean lands, was cut to shreds.

105

Few calamities have fallen upon settled and civilized areas so awe-inspiring or so swift as the armed passage of these Gothic and German hordes. In country areas which did not lie in the direct path of invading armies it was, no doubt, possible to continue living the old "Roman" life, as people can do today when they are temporarily by-passed by the mechanized aggressor. But such respite could not last indefinitely. A world-civilization without safe communications, without regularity in commerce or administration, rotted away into small sections; and these gradually let slip the habits and conventions of Roman culture until the arts of peace, buried beneath the mounting pile of fear and poverty, were almost forgotten, and western Europe entered the feudal stage in which land-occupation was dependent on the will of the local lord.

Among the many arts which were now abruptly cut off was that of coin-design. For a thousand years artists in Greece and Rome had been engraving dies which were very often distinguished and sometimes of exquisite quality. Within a century the long continued aptitude withered and died. It was not simply that the Graeco-Roman idiom was deliberately abandoned: in Italy, indeed, the artistic traditions of coinage were kept alive for a long time by the pale and powerless emperors who kept futile court at Ravenna, and both in Italy and elsewhere invading kings, quickly conscious of the vast economic prestige of Roman idiom in coinage, sedulously copied its main characteristics on the imitative money which they themselves minted. The truth was that highly trained engravers, practised in a continuous tradition, and capable of skilful and delicate work, could no longer be found: Gothic and German idiom in design, strong and even harsh though not necessarily always unpleasing in itself, failed to find artists who could represent it with much more skill than that possessed by a normally ingenious metal-smith. In that dark age of vast nomadic aggression the cycle of experiment and discovery began again: although the actual convention of minting money remained unbroken men had to find out afresh, as the Greeks had had to find out first, how to design and mint it well.

The conditions, indeed, were similar to those of early Greece in a number of ways. The Roman imperial coinage, over the centuries, had grown into a great and complex monetary structure, with an immense volume of coins minted every year, by an army of operatives each skilled in a specialist branch of work, at a number of centralized mints closely administered by the central government. But this elaborate system was destroyed, in the west, by the fragmentation of the western provinces, and coinage from the fifth century onwards became more narrowly regional, or even local, in character—the prerogative of provincial kings, of towns still more or less independent, and of bishops. At the same time its volume was very sharply reduced: in an age of flux and turmoil comparatively little silver and bronze was minted, and the principal object was to continue striking gold as an inter-regional and international currency corresponding to the almost universal silver of the Greek city-states. The conditions in which a sparing coinage, mainly in gold, was produced for a restricted number of consumers were substantially those of the early Greek mints with their initially small output of silver; and just as the early Greek mints were staffed by men who combined the functions of the smith and the engraver, not yet being specialized artist-engravers, so too the collapse of Roman power in the west led to the appearance of "monetarii"—moneyers, men who could engrave dies, though without any pretensions to style and with no understanding of plastic treatment at all, and who understood the technical process of striking the coins from the dies. In other words the sculptural idiom in the engraving of coin-dies, which the Greeks had elaborated with such magnificence and the Romans transmuted and adapted, was now entirely lost: it was enough if dies could be engraved with a pattern rendered in a simple, flat, linear style—a style in which technical skill was at a discount. From the fifth to the seventh century there was hardly a mint in western Europe which

107

could produce a coin combining elegance in conception with beauty of execution.

Nevertheless, there were new influences at work; and these, either separately or in union, were ultimately to foster the glories of medieval art in coinage. The late Roman coinage itself had shown that "classical" motifs were effectively worked out and that they no longer served as a proper vehicle for the thought and imagination of the best engravers: the flat and delicate relief of the best of the fourth-century pieces had made it obvious that artists were increasingly interested in the formalism of pattern as a means of filling the field of a coin, and that they were ready to abandon the highly plastic and sculptural idiom which sought to turn a coin into a miniature relief. In the Eastern empire, which under the sway of Byzantium was to perpetuate the traditions of Christian Rome against the mounting pressure of Islam for a thousand years, an artistic formalism was developed which drew immense subjective power from the still gravity of its religious content and from the skilful use of decorative regularity in pattern (below, pp. 124 ff.). From the steppes of eastern Europe and from the northern peoples came other new influences equally capable of forming attractive "surface patterns" for coins engraved in linear style and low relief— twining tendrils and writhing animals and interlacing knots and many other designs of a half-abstract, half-representational character, showing that same love of balanced curves that had been the beauty of Celtic art before. With Europe in flux these varied influences were constantly interlaced and blended; and when at last the years of invasion and movement were succeeded by an age of consolidation, in which new and stable kingdoms and principalities began to emerge, the process of cross-fertilization revealed its first results in coinage design almost wholly different from that of the western Roman Empire two centuries earlier.

Yet the re-birth of any deliberately artistic tradition in coinage was terribly slow. During the fifth and sixth centuries the western areas of Gaul and Spain, whether dominated by invading peoples or dragging out a Roman twilight in local autonomy, produced no coin of artistic merit at all. In either case, though for different reasons, Roman idiom was conscientiously followed until, sterile in conception and uncouth in execution, it sank to almost unrecognizable depths. In Italy itself there were occasional flashes of something better. Theodoric the Ostrogoth produced a gold medallion (66) with a superb Romano-Gothic facing portrait. Theodahad (A.D. 534–6), his nephew, was a lover of the ancient learning and, after he had deposed and then killed the talented queen Amalasuntha with whom he shared the Roman throne, he produced—in the short span remaining to him—a bronze coinage with portraits (65) most finely conceived and modelled with a subtlety and depth unknown for many years before. The king is shown beardless, but wearing a moustache— the break with all previous tradition is immediately evident. His hair is combed down in a straight fringe over his forehead and falls, slightly incurled, to his neck. Upon his head sits a closed, arched crown, with jewels in the band and the arches, presenting us with the image not of any quasi-Roman emperor but of a Gothic king. The relief is high: the workmanship is much more than competent; and the character is rendered with complete realism untouched by any trace of Byzantine formalism. Not all examples of this portrait are equally pleasing, and it is likely that Theodahad commanded the services of at least one master-engraver whose work was afterwards copied by much inferior men. It was nearly two centuries before Italy again produced coins of such great distinction, and by then the influence of Byzantium was paramount, with all its still elegance and formal grace: the Lombard dukes of Beneventum, indeed, were powerful intermediaries between the civilizations of Byzantium on the one hand and Carolingian France on the other. These dukes did not choose to put their own portraits on the coins which they struck, but that of the current emperor at Byzantium instead. Thus Romoald II (A.D. 706–731) represented the portrait of Justinian II—a full-face portrait in flat, low relief, executed in a linear style and without any modelling at all. Although there is a ceremonial stillness in this facing figure there is no stiffness, and the feeling is sensitive and lively, not least because the low relief in which the die was engraved enabled the artist to make full use of an elaborate pattern of strong lines in head-dress, curls, necklace and drapery. Here once more it would be safe to postulate the presence of master-artists whose work formed a model for officially appointed imitators.

In northern Europe, distant from the influence of either Rome or Byzantium, new idioms arose and new styles prevailed, infused with the strength—sometimes harsh, sometimes more delicate—of the Anglo-Saxon peoples who from the end of the third century had been moving steadily westward from Scandinavia and Denmark into the Low Countries and England. The first truly English coin to be minted at London (it bears the inscription LONDVNIV on the reverse) must have been made by order of that Bishop Mellitus whom St. Augustine appointed to the see of London in A.D. 604 "to preach to the province of the East Saxons who are divided from Kent by the river Thames: their metropolis is the city of London, the mart of many peoples coming by sea and land." And it need not be doubted that it bears the bishop's portrait (67)—an uncouth linear outline of a fully facing tonsured head, with a stole, its ends adorned by crosses, around his neck. And yet, though the technique is so uncouth, this portrait possesses a fine power almost amounting to grandeur. It is right to remember the difficulties inherent in portraiture at this time. The advent and constant spread of Christianity had long since driven out the impersonal representation of anthropomorphic deities so dear to the Greek masters and their early Roman successors. The success of the Roman "personal" portrait had depended upon the ability of highly trained engravers to cut their dies in an elaborately plastic idiom. And now, although the need for individualized portraits of kings and prelates still remained, this plastic skill had disappeared: the storm of European invasion had swept

110

BARBARIAN INHERITORS OF ROME

65 Theodahad (p. 109), 66 Theodoric (p. 109)

EARLY ANGLO-SAXON STYLES

67 London (pp. 110, 113), 68, 69 Offa of Mercia
(pp. 115 ff.), 70 London (?) (p. 113)

away the inherited tradition that went with the mass-production of a highly centralized coinage. Thus the engraver who was required to represent Mellitus looked at his subject with eyes uninfluenced by any current trend or fashion, and saw it with a freedom comparable to that with which the ancient Britons had viewed the Gaulish "Apollo-head" as a prototype for their own designs. His clear, simple vision—the rich gift of all "primitives"—showed him a thin oval face, with eyes deep-set under a heavy fringe of hair. This, and no more, his unskilled hand and unelaborate instruments could represent; and the resultant portrait therefore enjoys the simplicity, directness and highly concentrated integrity of all young art. It is no masterpiece, but it is of outstanding interest. It transcended the dispassionate symbolism of late Roman coinage: it was free from the elegant regularity of current Byzantine work; and its plain forms express eloquently what the artist felt.

But engravers were arising in northern Europe who could attempt more elaborate work and whose conception was at once more fluent and more delicate. The men who made the little silver sceattas, either in France and the Low Countries or in south-eastern England, possessed a remarkably strong sense of design and a great aptitude for making that design conform to the small area offered by a coin-die. In portraiture, when they undertook it, they achieved a charm which owes as much to its essentially decorative treatment as it does to its simple forms. This is still the work of "primitives", but it is already infused by the excitement of coming alive, as when the early Greek artists found means of suggesting that the eyes and mouth possessed expression. The small head (70), placed well to the side of the coin, looks fixedly at the goblet which a hand holds up. For all its temporary immobility we know that the mouth will soon drink, that the head will incline, that the hair—conventionally rendered in a few formal strokes—will fall about the face. This little portrait is full of feeling, for it inevitably suggests a range of human activity which can easily be anticipated in the imagination.

Nevertheless, pictorial designs—apart from portraits—waned in most parts of Europe from the seventh century onward. The decorative quality of good and bold lettering was something that nearly every engraver could achieve: only artists of outstanding ability could conceive pictorial subjects in a form suitable for coinage, which denied all opportunity for the display of those ample, ribbon-like bands of highly complex ornament so dear to the early illuminators. Upon lettering, therefore, subtly arranged around some form of cross, sometimes plain, sometimes highly decorated, the moneyers of northern Europe were to rely for their reverse-designs for many centuries to come. Technically they chose an easy task. A moneyer who possessed a small number of punches, their ends bearing the strokes I, ᶜ, ᴄ, ı, ●, ○, could engrave from these, in combination where necessary, any letter of the alphabet that was needed; and it was even possible for an inferior, unskilled moneyer to build up a "portrait" also from some such simple apparatus. It must be remembered that from the seventh century onward European coinage multiplied in volume. Thin silver pennies were poured out in growing numbers by many kingdoms and cities, and the convention whereby local gold- or silversmiths could coin under licence—so long as their basic designs were officially approved—naturally led to a long epoch of coinage in which technical skill sank to a merely elementary level and beauty of conception was simply not considered. Coinage, for the time being, was no more than an economic convenience, and the classical tradition of fine workmanship and imagination was wholly lost. Some moneyers might be more skilled than others; but hardly any could rise above the simple task of making letter-patterns—in reality, little more than signets.

The occasional emergence of first-class work in this period from A.D. 700 onwards therefore strikes the eye with double emphasis: in such cases we see the clear sign of desire in high places that coinage should earn its place in a competitive world not only by the purity of its metal but also by the excellence of its design. Charlemagne himself provides one such instance. From his father Pepin he inherited a tradition of coin-design that was crude and sterile to a degree, but by the time of his death he had trained his artists to represent him in all the majesty of Roman imperial idiom—a small portrait head, wreathed, with draped shoulders. More remarkable still was the case of King Offa of Mercia (A.D. 757–96). Offa had spent some time at the court of Charlemagne, and after his conquest of Kent at the battle of Otford in A.D. 774 he determined to put the traditional resources of the Canterbury mint to the task of producing a coinage not less splendid than that of Charlemagne. The result was a coinage which, in its freedom of conception, its technical skill and its aesthetic quality was one of the finest England has ever known.

It is not easy to analyse its peculiar beauty, for, as is the case with nearly all outstandingly good works of art, that beauty is something more than the accumulation of individually good elements, lying rather in their effortless and wholly successful combination, as is shown indeed by those less skilled moneyers of Offa who produced coins of interest but not of eminent quality. But the best of his moneyers commanded—and the miracle was that they commanded it so quickly and fully—a mastery of technical methods and the enjoyment of the most delicate taste. Eadhun's portrait of Offa (68) serves as an admirable example. It was engraved eccentrically on the die, rather in the manner of the little Saxon "drinking" portrait previously noted (above, p. 113) on a sceatta. But Eadhun had more space to play with, for Offa was coining silver pennies larger than the sceattas; and he took full advantage of it. The portrait rises to the border of the coin: the hair, elegantly arranged in puffed rolls, catches the light in a way that renders the portrait airy and graceful. In the modelling of the features there is no great detail; but they are represented sculpturally, the rounded jaw swelling up from the surface of the coin, the lips firm and sensitive. As a foil to these gentle, cultured features the artist delineated the shoulder drapery in the hard and conventional

115

strokes, suggesting armour and the like, which had become normal since the later issues of Rome. In his final touch Eadhun showed that he was as much a master of purely decorative idiom as he was of the lost art of portraiture, for in front of the king's head appears his name in clear and handsome letters of great distinction, picked out and adorned with arrangements of dots. In this attractive detail the art of the illuminator was added to that of the portraitist; and the whole design stands out for its grace and beauty, so variously combined and so skilfully balanced.

Eadhun, as is obvious, must have used tools far superior to those with which earlier Saxon moneyers had plied their trade. Not for him a set of simple punches: his die demanded, above all, that the area of the face should be laboriously cut into it, exactly as the master engravers of Greece and Rome, scorning a simply engraved linear portrait, had also done. But the linear style which moneyers (content to work in a single plane of relief) had adopted since the collapse of the Roman Empire in the west was itself raised to new and splendid heights by Offa's artists. Among them was Eadberht, who, in designing a non-portrait obverse for Offa, made exclusive use of the decorative idiom which Eadhun had employed in his own lettering, and built it up into a handsome and elaborate pattern (69). Within the circle of the coin he set a lozenge with curving sides; and within this again a second circle; and within this second circle a decorated cross which emphasized all the contrasting stresses of the other balanced elements. A lesser artist could easily have done as much, and produced a purely mechanical design—the sort of pattern which builds itself up automatically under the eye of anyone interested in the aesthetic relationship of squares and circles. But Eadberht gave fluency and rhythm to the pattern by disposing the letters OFFA+REX in pairs, flanked by little groups of dots, within the curving sides of the lozenge; and the masterly result was the immediate livening of the regular pattern.

Offa's coinage will always provoke deep interest. It flowered suddenly, with no apparent introductory development: its beauty died, with Offa's death, equally suddenly, leaving to subsequent generations a number of motifs to be imitated by unskilled moneyers, in whose hands they degenerated wretchedly. Clearly such a phenomenon reflects the desires and tastes of the king himself, who must have built up and encouraged new artistic traditions, exactly as was done by so many of the city-states of Greece and by those Roman Emperors, like Hadrian and Antoninus Pius, who fed an increasing technical skill with a supply of new and stimulating conceptions. For it was in conception, no less than in skill, that Offa's artists differed so fundamentally from those before and after them. They wrought intricately with their imagination, creating what was much more than merely charming and much less than undisciplined fantasy; and they departed absolutely from the "Roman" tradition embraced by Charlemagne and followed by Louis the Pious, whose famous portrait-piece, with all its fine plastic treatment and its vivid suggestion of the emperor's personal features, did little more than re-create the past glories of Rome and was unable even to show a command of firm and regularly balanced lettering. Reverence for the idiom of imperial Rome was not enough to evoke the masterly technique of Roman engravers.

In England, therefore, after Offa's reign and in western Europe as a whole the art of making beautiful coins was lost, and was not in general recovered until the thirteenth century. But in various states of Germany a determined effort was made in the twelfth century to overcome the technical difficulties which had by then for so long obstructed the free development and imaginative expression of the moneyer's art. The peoples of northern Europe had been accustomed, in much earlier periods, to "coining" thin discs of metal which bore a perfect impression on one side only, the other side showing no more than a "ghost" of this impression; and pieces of this kind had been used as personal ornaments. Now the same technique was employed for coinage proper. The record of coinage in western Europe since the sixth century A.D. had shown that, with only the rarest exceptions, die-engravers had lost the ability of the ancients to carve dies, in complex detail, which were capable of impressing coin-blanks in clear and emphatic relief. But, granted the desire to improve the appearance of coinage, by increasing the height and variety of its relief as a means of securing bolder and more elaborate design, the wafer-thin disc of metal offered the chance of progress. In order to produce "bracteate" coinage, as it is called, a moneyer would need to engrave one highly finished die, carved to considerable depth and as complex as he wished to make it. Upon this die the very thin blank would be placed; and then, upon the blank, a second die which did no more than repeat the principal lines of design of the main die. A hammer-blow would drive the wafer of soft silver well into the main die, and a coin would thus be produced which, though unusually fragile, at least bore upon one side a high-relief design of considerable elaboration. It is noticeable, moreover, that these bracteates were made in a size which gave die-engravers full scope for the imaginative development of design.

Thus there arose quite suddenly, and continued for some generations, an entirely novel school of art in coinage. It was a school which must be called essentially "primitive": its technique was sometimes rough, its treatment of the human figure was often perfunctory, and it hardly attained the pitch of true portraiture. But to say this is merely to repeat what might well be said of the beginnings of Greek coinage, and it is wise not to be reminded in advance of the infinitely more polished beauties which Renaissance coinage was so soon to bring. The achievement of these early German artists was, indeed, magnificent and memorable. Art is no mere matter of technique: the heart that gives it life is to be sought rather in the artist's eyes and imagination, from which comes the individual quality of his conceptions. And the conceptions on these bracteates are astonishingly varied. Primarily religious, the bracteates picture—for the first time in western Europe—the background of Christian tradition and chivalry with a simple pathos that is deeply moving.

Stephen, robed and haloed, suffers martyrdom by stoning (71): his head is conventionally tilted, partly perhaps in agony, partly to gaze up at the sun-burst of Christ's glory above him, and he raises a hand, perhaps as much to bless as to plead. All around stand the tormentors, their arms filled with stones, some of which are even now bringing the saint to his knees; and those who stone him break, with their outstretched arms, the border of the design, as Stephen's feet do also, thus giving the design a minute but subtle suggestion of the extension of the whole fearful scene on a scale far larger and more turbulent than the coin itself can allow. The same martyr—the patron saint of Halberstadt—is seen on another coin (73) in his arched tomb, stones heaped above him, while angels fly aloft holding up his haloed likeness. At Magdeburg we see St. Maurice, dressed in full medieval armour: at Nordhausen, St. Eustace who, in an exceptionally graceful composition rendered in the finest style (74), sits holding a cross while the Abbess Berta kneels before him, a slender figure of pious humility, her hands raised in beseeching prayer and her eyes cast down.

The vivid pleasure to be drawn from these splendid designs lies partly in the sincerity with which the artists conceived them, partly in the willingness with which the artists broke so abruptly from the currently prevailing traditions, partly in the passionately decorative sense which they showed. They were, as is obvious, stimulated by both the subject-matter and also the style of painting and sculpture of the same period; and their special excellence is to be seen in the skill and exquisite taste with which they adapted large "pictorial" compositions to the narrow confines of a coin. Indeed, their fondness for ample design and their determination to secure, at all costs, a true feeling of depth and distance in this tiny field prompted them to make an experiment in the treatment of the circle. It was to be seen in the design of St. Stephen entombed, already noticed above, where the circular field of the coin is divided in the approximate ratio of $\frac{2}{3} : \frac{1}{3}$ by a curved band which serves to separate the scene of the tomb from that of the angels in heaven above. It is seen in many other bracteates as well, as, for instance, in that of Henry archbishop of Erfurt in the middle of the twelfth century (72). Here St. Martin occupies the upper and larger panel of the design, flanked on either side by turrets; below the curving band appears Henry, his head aslant in the "expressionist" idiom of the time—analogous to the "archaic smile" of early Greek figures—and his hands raised in blessing or prayer. It was a bold innovation of great vision and interest to depart from the old formula which had taught that a coin-design should be clearly balanced on the centre of the field. By the occasional and judicious use of the new layout these early German artists achieved a panoramic interest which few coinages could equal.

Elsewhere in Europe the art of coinage was at a standstill. The sense of pictorial design was lost: the aptitude for portraiture, which could revive momentarily and so brilliantly under an Offa, and which in any case depended upon an artist's sculptural ability in cutting his dies, seemed also to be gone; and technique in general was poor and coarse. Only in the south was there the occasional flash of noble conception, as in the gold "augustale" of Frederic II of the Two Sicilies in the early thirteenth century (here the grandeur was borrowed, through the monetary idiom of Louis the Pious and Charlemagne, from that of imperial Rome), and the gold of Charles I of Anjou, where this Roman grandeur is being gracefully translated into the guise of medieval kingship (82). The artist who designed this last coin was on the threshold of the Renaissance, when the true test of skill was finally recognized as lying in the polished and perfect representation of the human figure and human features in a decorative setting.

At the moment when the Renaissance opened upon Europe, and as Pisanello designed his famous medallic portrait of John Palaeologus, the twilight emperor of Byzantium, the Byzantine empire itself was within a few years of its collapse in the face of the Turks, and John's own coinage had descended

CONCEPTION AND TECHNIQUE IN MEDIEVAL
GERMANY

EARLIER BYZANTINE PORTRAITURE

75 | 76
77 | 78   75 Heraclius (p. 124 f.), 76–78 Justinian II (p. 125 f.),
79   79 Leo III (p. 126 f.)

to the uttermost depth of wretchedness, barren and miserable in conception and coarse in design. Seldom have the fortunes of a great power been so clearly reflected in the changing form of its coinage; and seldom has antithesis spoken more eloquently than when John's Byzantine coinage and John's Italian-made medal, in contrast, declare eastern collapse and western resurrection. Nevertheless, the record of Byzantium in the annals of civilization was an astonishing one. When the western Empire, based on Italy, crumpled before the invaders in the middle of the fifth century, that of the East, founded on Constantinople, stood firm. At the time of Justinian's accession in A.D. 527 everything that lay west of a line drawn from north-west Greece to Cyrenaica seemed lost to Roman and Christian tradition. Three-quarters of a century later, Byzantium had manfully reconquered from the barbarians much that they had won: her sea-power had reclaimed the Adriatic, with Venice and Ravenna, southern Italy and Sicily, and even Rome itself; and further west Sardinia and Corsica and southern Spain and Carthaginian Africa were recovered. The achievement was colossal and its spiritual importance immense, for in regaining so much of what had been lost in the central and western Mediterranean Byzantium was acting as the direct successor of Rome herself and was propagating a Christian tradition far more elaborate than any which Rome had propounded. Justinian's policy, dictated from Constantinople, where culture was all the more diverse and motley from its being the meeting-place of east and west, Greek and Roman, pagan and Christian, was founded squarely on the view that church and state, though formally distinct, were one and the same in actual practice. Combining in himself the functions of emperor and head of the Church, Justinian paid equal heed to both interests; and thus his capital became an essentially religious centre, where the practice of religion, the complex discussion of theology and a ruthless resistance to paganism and heresy were much more the matters of everyday concern than anything else. The wars of Justinian were indeed crusades.

Religion, accordingly, became the almost exclusive theme of Byzantine art and thus—because coinage, in the classical tradition, was regarded as a section of socially applied art—impregnated the coins as well. In the late Roman coinage of the west, Christian elements of design had multiplied in the century and a half after Constantine the Great. The early Byzantine coinage, down to Justinian's accession, made little change in the old Roman idiom in this respect; but from Justinian onwards it shows an increasingly strong hieratic feeling. Profile heads gave way almost entirely to facing heads; and these facing figures confront us in all the solemn majesty of religious eminence, their heads haloed, their hands holding the crosses, orbs and sceptres which marked Caesars who were near-Popes. The Roman figure of winged Victory, with wreath and palm, had long since turned into a Christian angel holding a cross; and with Tiberius II (A.D. 578–82) the cross on a high platform of steps became a very commonly used design.

At length, with Heraclius (A.D. 610-41), the Byzantine coinage began to attain the peak of its characteristic beauty. This brilliant figure found an empire gravely diminished from that which Justinian had reconquered and built up. Constantinople was again little more than the capital of a kingdom consisting of the Balkans and Asia Minor—a kingdom dangerously menaced by Persian forces, who actually succeeded in capturing Jerusalem and carrying off, temporarily, the True Cross. Total reform and reorganization were the prelude to a new series of holy wars; and as a part of this process Heraclius, as is evident, encouraged the die-engravers of his time to depart from the old conventions which had fettered originality ever since Rome fell 150 years previously. By the middle of his reign a new school of imperial artistry had developed, working in a style which may truly be called the early medieval style of Byzantium. It was fine, formal, statuesque and decorative, and attained to something very near genuine portraiture, as on the gold coins which show the emperor with his young son and colleague, Heraclius Constantine (75). The emperor, described elsewhere as a broadly built man with fine eyes and yellow hair, faces us in a portrait by no means devoid of modelling. His crown, topped by a cross, sits upon thick hair curling gently round his cheeks: the beard is moderately full, and grows high on the cheeks to meet the falling locks of hair. Beside him, in a lower, miniature portrait befitting his junior status, appears the young son: here the hair is curled and rolled above the cheeks; and the narrower, more pointed chin speaks of youthfulness. The whole composition is strangely unbalanced owing to the imperial formula which set the emperor literally in a higher plane than any junior colleague: the artist himself, feeling this, attempted to right the balance—though not altogether successfully—by inserting a cross as a decorative symbol in the empty space above the heads. Nevertheless this is a work of deep feeling, executed with a delicate strength and a fine precision not seen on the coinage since the days of Rome; and the artist, while not representing the true features of the imperial colleagues, has expressed their personalities partly by their ceremonial insignia, partly by emphasizing those physical characteristics which were widely known at the time. The interest of his work lies in its technical polish. This is developed to a point at which it might as easily have turned to a greater formalism on the one hand or, on the other, to a new and full exploitation of naturalism in the rendering of humanity—a naturalism which had effectively disappeared from the imperial coinage after the reign of Constantine.

And these, in fact, were the contrasting idioms most clearly to be seen in Byzantine coinage for the next 300 years, the contrasts being from time to time sharpened by the great iconoclastic movement begun by Leo III (A.D. 717–41) and abrogated a century later under Michael III. When Justinian II, whose coins called him the "servant of Christ," first introduced the head of Christ as a design for the coinage soon after A.D. 685, this was often represented in a naturalistic style strongly at variance with the imperial portrait of the time. For while Justinian's features are shown in a thin and priestly style (76), with a narrow, clipped fringe of beard framing the austere oval of his face, the portrait of Christ (inscribed "King of Kings") is conceived with a freedom of expression which can point only to the existence of paintings or sculptures, of an earlier or more naturalistic style, which the coin-designers copied. Christ's head (77) is set against the Cross: the hair flows free, almost unkempt, around a face in which eyes and mouth possess a genuine intensity of feeling; and the drapery—the flowing robe cast around the shoulders—contrasts strongly with Justinian's imperial vestment. But a second form of Christ-portrait must also have existed as a basis for coin-design. In this the divine head is formalized (78): no longer do we see the long-haired, full-bearded Saviour, with all the suggestion of the years of toil and the agony of suffering, but instead the divine counterpart of the emperor himself—a delicately pointed face lightly fringed with beard, its noble brow surmounted by elaborately curled hair.

Such coins, although their technique was not up to the level which had characterized the artists of Greece and Rome, were nevertheless works of high competence, and in their sense of design they were far superior to much that Rome, and even Greece, had produced. The artists, boldly taking over the facing head as the standard element of design, succeeded in delineating it, with just the slightest suggestion of modelling, in such a way that the grave men who look out from these thin, flat, elegant coins possess astonishing dignity and personality. In the world of Byzantine art, replete with ceremony and formality, symbolism was well understood; but the symbolism of these coin-artists was not so austere as to be repellent, nor was their technique so simple as to make impossible demands on the beholder. These portraits themselves conveyed impressions which the beholder's own emotions could suitably amplify.

The dualism of style—naturalism vying with formalism—which marked the reign of Justinian II was seen equally clearly under Leo III, the iconoclast, whose coinage banished

126

the representation of Christ. Leo's portrait appears sometimes in the austere and emaciated treatment seen already for Justinian: at other times, and within the same mint, it is accorded a highly realistic treatment of great vitality and exuberance (79), showing the emperor with a rotund, well-bearded face in which the thick firm lips and widely open, heavy-lidded eyes convey a very strong impression of personality. It is clear that two schools of coin-designers existed side by side. And of these two schools the formalists carried the day, presumably because the mass-preparation of dies cut in a flat, linear style was very much easier than that of dies which required the modeller's art in addition to the engraver's. Occasionally the two styles were combined to achieve a flash of magnificence which argues the activity of quite exceptionally good artists. Thus at the end of the eighth century, when western Europe was beginning to experiment with new ideas in portraiture, Constantine VI produced a coin of outstanding quality (80). Formal treatment is evident in the long, thin, regular outlines of the face framed by tenuous and stylized locks of hair; but the artist who made this die was not afraid to model the emperor's features, nor to give to his eyes an expression of dignity and restraint. But from this time onwards the general tendency lay away from the direction of human realism. More and more, artists were fascinated by the attraction of designs in which decorative pattern was the chief element. This could be gained by engraving dies which consisted of nothing but highly ornamental lettering, line upon line, from top to bottom. Or, when the iconoclastic movement ended with Michael III in the middle of the ninth century and the sacred likenesses returned to the coinage, the artists could begin to work up such themes as Christ seated in glory, or the Virgin Mary, praying, or crowning the emperor below the outstretched hand of God (81), or—perhaps most surprising of all—the emperor's miniature portrait set within a medallion at the heart of the limbs of an elaborately adorned cross.

Such designs as these were executed in a hard, clear, neat

127

style and in reasonably high relief. In conception they show originality; but artistically their interest is confined to their decorative sense. These are themes which the religious paintings and mosaics of the time had made familiar to the die-engravers; and the engravers, in adapting them for coinage, added nothing by which they could show—as the bracteate-designers were so soon to show—that the special problems of coin-design had been considered on their own merits. Like the die-engravers of the Roman Republican period, they took a given theme, confined it within a circle and reproduced it, thus cramped, as the design for a coin. Of matters of proportion and balance they were careless or unaware; and, free from the necessity of creating any novel conceptions by the very abundance of ready-made themes in contemporary art-forms of different kinds, they allowed their obviously fine powers of delicate and decorative engraving to coarsen and degenerate in the last four centuries of Byzantine independence. It was, nevertheless, on this late Byzantine capacity for fine engraving and decorative form that the early Renaissance artists were soon to draw so fully.

Greek coinage had traversed the indisputable peak of its glory over a period of about three centuries. Then, after a lapse of two hundred years more, the Roman imperial coinage put forth its choicest aspect for another four centuries. In each the true source of greatness was clear. The artists were above all concerned with human form and human expression, and they tended to make coin-dies of a size which allowed a skilful man to make the most of this subject-matter by adding the sculptor's art to that of the engraver. After the fall of the Roman empire in the west and the incursion of great forces from unromanized tracts of Europe the Graeco-Roman tradition quickly withered and perished, or left— at the most—an empty shell to be imitated by a Charlemagne or a Louis the Pious. No longer did artists look at men simply as men: instead, the medieval conception of kingship began to obtrude itself, and against the magnificently individual portraits of Theodoric and Theodahad, re-creating the past splendour of classical portraiture in Gothic vein, we have to set a subsequent series of increasingly stylized representations of monarchs who—with the exception of Offa—are shown with the robes and crowns and sceptres and orbs which, more than any personal features, mark them as what they are. The ceremonial splendour of royal power, rather than the personal qualities to be looked for in royalty, engaged the attention of artists in the darkened Middle Ages: in Byzantium, with comparatively few exceptions, that same ceremonial splendour, in the aspect of the emperor as servant of God, provided the same stimulus. It was the peculiar achievement of Renaissance Europe that, without losing this sense of splendour, it re-discovered and again expressed the dominant interest of human personality, and, in doing so, once more attained to the technical perfection of the classical artists.

CHAPTER VII

The Return of Naturalism

THE die-engravers who had been working in the chaos of Europe and in the still radiant and vigorous Byzantine Empire from the fifth century onwards, with the brief exception of the "bracteate" artists of Germany, made no advance in the technical methods of coining which the early Greeks had first developed. Their dies, carved with essentially the same instruments the Greeks had used, were still hammer-struck by workmen upon the coin-blanks laid between them; and this simple manual operation, so far from stimulating artists to achieve novelty in technique by increasing or varying the planes of relief, in which Greek and Roman masters had in turn excelled, depressed the creative instinct, as we have seen, until designers were content with little more than linear patterns. Designers, indeed, were by now simply moneyers—men responsible for coining the metal entrusted to them into a recognizable form. The vision of beauty and originality which beset the ancients had for the most part faded; and as it faded there came—what would have profoundly surprised the ancients—a contentment if a standard pattern, normally lettering round a cross, could be followed. It is curious to reflect how coinage, after being so brilliantly elevated from the simple technique of the seal-maker by the Greeks, returned to that same standard—plain, unadventurous, unimaginative and often unpictorial—after a lapse of twelve centuries. Perhaps there is both warning and encouragement in such a phenomenon. Old techniques, in their day the vehicle of magnificent conceptions, can too easily encourage the imitative and banal in the hands of those who are no more than craftsmen. But when a new technique

130

LATER BYZANTINE AND FRENCH MEDIEVAL
PORTRAITURE

$$\frac{\frac{80}{81}}{82}$$ 80 Constantine VI (p. 127), 81 John I Zimisces (p. 127),
82 Charles I of Anjou (p. 120)

83
PISANELLO
Medal of Gianfrancesco Gonzaga (obverse) (pp. 138, 141)

84

PISANELLO

Medal of Gianfrancesco Gonzaga (reverse) (p. 141)

PISANELLO

85, 86 Medal of Leonello d'Este (p. 141)

is developed, as the Greeks developed that of making dies for high-relief coinage, a whole new world of vision and variety is opened up, and master-artists are generally ready to take advantage of it.

It was in the fifteenth century that the supremely important moment of new technique and fresh vision arrived, stimulating artists to forsake stale and jaded idiom for something which afforded them full opportunity for penetrating observation and varied expression. And we are on firm historical ground in assigning the revolutionary change to Antonio Pisano of Verona, surnamed Pisanello, who lived from about 1395 to 1455. Pisanello first won reputation—and in his own day—as a consummately skilful painter of portraits and of animals, working in Pavia, Mantua, Venice, Ferrara and Rome for those many noble figures in whom, with the change from medieval feudalism to a society of individuals, there arose the burning desire for personal fame and glorification. This prodigy was scarcely more than twenty-five years old when he had attained to the foremost rank as a painter. In his forties, when he was already mature in the painter's art and totally familiar with all the discipline of a new representational idiom, he turned his attention to the making of medals.

In the history of monetary art down to Pisanello's day medal-like pieces had from time to time appeared—the great Greek "medallion" of Acragas (p. 35) (23, 24), the splendid Roman "medallions" made for Hadrian and Antoninus Pius (pp. 92 ff.) (52–4), and those later Roman "medallions" of Constantius and the fourth-century emperors (pp. 100, 104) (59–61, 64). Some of these, for example the piece of Acragas and the fourth-century Roman pieces, were coin-multiples in medallic form, by which is meant that their artistry and elaboration rise far above what was usually thought necessary for coinage proper. The Hadrianic and Antonine pieces were more truly medallic in the sense that they were not intended to play a part in the monetary system, being designed—and with a careful, loving art—simply for purposes of presentation or commemoration. All, however, possessed one feature in common: they were the official productions of officially controlled mints, and their spirit was essentially the spirit of state control. In addition, they were all struck from metal dies which the artists, as in the case of coinage proper, had carved; and because they were struck in this way their size—though it had considerably exceeded that of many normal coins—had been very severely limited owing to the technical difficulties involved in striking by hand. None were of really ample dimensions, and consequently the opportunities of truly sculptural representation by the artists who engraved the dies were proportionately limited.

Thus Pisanello, a painter of great genius, accustomed to working in a size much greater than that of a gem or private seal, and living in an age when portraits of noble and famous men were increasingly popular, devised what was apparently a new medallic technique. He did not engrave and carve metal dies. Instead, he modelled his designs in relief in wax—a material which allowed and indeed encouraged the most delicate treatment; and from the wax relief-models sunk moulds were prepared, from which the medals were finally cast, usually in bronze, the colour of which lends itself with special perfection to the caster's art, or in lead. The advantages of this technique, practised by such a master of wax and bronze as was Pisanello, were obvious. The relief of the designs could be high, and the medals could be made in a size far larger than could be struck from dies by hand. Moreover, such was the exquisite fineness of his modelling and such his skill in the preparation of his moulds and the pouring in of his molten metal, that these cast medals were produced with a surface texture of a new and splendid beauty. For centuries the world had been accustomed to the hard, sharp, bright appearance of metal hammer-pressed between dies. Now men could see medals which, unless they were specially chased and burnished, did not shine. Their surface, like that of the human skin, was neither rough nor smooth. It caught the light gently, and held it sensitively; and the relation between light and shadow at once acquired a new significance.

These were all developments which, at a time of astonishing aesthetic experiment and enjoyment, would be exciting enough, providing as they did so strong a contrast to the masterpieces of ancient coinage which were already being avidly collected by connoisseurs. But there was much more to Pisanello than a mere revolution in technique. For the new ability to mould, delicately and exactly, in a sensitive plastic medium allowed him and his successors to do what had been denied by the previous degenerate processes of die-cutting. What the eye could see the hand could once more represent, as in the days of Greece and Rome. The stiff, cramped Gothic idiom in coin-design, while it undoubtedly owed much to a tradition of thought which ran counter to that of classical humanism, was not less the result of inability to cut dies in a sharply engraved and highly finished form. But now Pisanello's wax-model technique encouraged softer, more fluid forms and three-dimensional feeling. Quite suddenly curves returned, in an abundance which is profoundly surprising and refreshing after some centuries of dominantly rectilinear style; and with the curves comes also the desire to treat a design once more as an essay in relief-composition, with all the sense of depth and distance which the great masters have always delighted in suggesting. And this, in its turn, meant that the artist's eye could analyse his subject-matter in meticulous detail. The Greek engravers, as we have seen, possessed the supremely important gift of bringing the keenest and most penetrating observation to bear upon the objects which they chose to represent, with a consequent realism that owes its interest to a spirit of truth combined with a passionate interest in ideal forms—the whole being momentarily isolated in space and time. Pisanello's work presents closely parallel characteristics; for, while the earthly trappings of his day belong to the modern and not to the ancient world, and thus suggest that his treatment too is unclassical, the fact remains that his concentration upon the

137

subject-matter was equally close and his preoccupation with ideal form equally constant.

His first medal, as is known, was made in 1438, when he modelled the portrait of John Palaeologus—that Byzantine Emperor, on a temporary visit to Italy, whose east-Mediterranean coinage displayed a technical and stylistic poverty which betokened the impending collapse of the Byzantine empire. In less than twenty years thereafter Pisanello completed between two and three dozen portrait-medals. It has rightly been remarked that, as a medallist, he attained at one stroke the summit of his art. There is naturally room for preference, and even possibly for criticism, in the formation of his designs, though his extant sketches show to what lengths of study and analysis he was prepared to go before committing a design to the strictly circular limits of a wax model. But in all these medals the technical mastery is profound, and in all we can see the new phenomenon—a return to absolute realism in human and animal forms. This realism, however, is controlled (as in the case of the Greeks) by the artist's ability to concentrate his observation upon an object in such a way as to make it selective in detail, simple in presentation, and universal in its feeling.

From the matchless series of Pisanello's medals three can be described in order to show this combination of realism and simplicity, together with the artist's obvious pleasure in working out new and experimental forms. First in date comes that of Gianfrancesco Gonzaga (83), first marquess of Mantua (1407–1444). The obverse portrait, at a single glance, presents us with many of the important elements in Pisanello's formula for portrait-medals. There is a deliberate contrast between the vertical stress of the portrait itself—a vivid masterpiece of shrewdly conceived realism, with its tight, lean features set on the thin and curving neck and crowned by the monstrous hat—and the horizontal stress of the inscription across the field. But the contrast is not brutal, as it would have been if Pisanello had left the medal without a border: curving bands of admirably proportioned lettering

87

PISANELLO

Medal of Domenico Malatesta (obverse) (p. 141)

88

PISANELLO

Medal of Domenico Malatesta (reverse) (p. 141 f.)

above and below impart a swing and circular rhythm to the whole design. For the young marquess Leonello d'Este of Ferrara he tried a different idiom (85). Here the head is larger, with a mere suggestion of the breast below the neck; and the artist has infused into Leonello's portrait, with its fantastic sea of waving hair, a deeper quality of character-observation. No inscription is allowed to cut the field, which is instead surrounded by a totally enclosed band of elegant lettering. In his portrait of Domenico Malatesta, lord of Cesena (1429–65), Pisanello showed a third treatment (87). In this the portrait—rendered with exquisite delicacy, and once more given its quota of interest by the proportions of the hair-mass—is of medium size, and descends to breast length: a horizontal inscription cuts across the field, but only a single semicircular letter-band is allowed, at the top. In each case balance has been worked out with almost mathematical accuracy, and the wonderfully satisfying proportion between space filled and space unfilled shows the sure touch of a genius.

The reverses of these medals, equally, are works of the utmost quality. All three are signed (as Pisanello always signed) "the work of Pisano the painter." It was as a painter that he saw his subjects, indeed, with all their solidity, depth and colour. But it was as a modeller that he transmuted these visible elements into relief. The Gonzaga reverse (84) suggests at least five planes of receding depth—sword upon thigh upon horse upon tail upon horse upon landscape; and with this there is the contrast of opposing directions, the one horse (its legs and hooves so cunningly accommodated to the shape of the medal) walking out of our sight to the left, the other disappearing into the distance lying infinitely ahead. Leonello d'Este's reverse (86) is plainly a *tour de force*: the triple-faced cherub is an exercise in the variation of planes, devised with no less amusement than skill. The Malatesta reverse (88) is perhaps the greatest of the three. Landscape peak and rock curve up, crescent-wise, on either side, repeating the bottom curve of the medal's own shape. In the midst

141

Domenico, fully armed, kneels before a Cross from which Christ's head hangs forward so heavily as to seem to bend in grace towards him. So much, alone, might have been fine design, with the Cross piercing an arched sky suggested by the curve of Pisanello's signature. But the artist wished to depict not only the wilderness of empty space but also the agony of time, and so, balancing the human group, inserted a great horse, tethered to a barren tree, its noble and well-rounded hindquarters facing us as it stands, patient, with only the slightest turn of its neck.

Pisanello's new technical methods enabled him to cast numerous examples of each of his medals. As a result, their beauty, both of conception and of production, at once became widely known, and schools of medallic artists arose in various Italian cities, the technique of casting being carried on with the utmost skill before it gave way, inevitably, to methods of hand-striking from dies carved by a rejuvenated artistry not seen since the days of Greece and Rome. It is doubtful if the simple perfection, the shrewd realism and the easy dignity of Pisanello's style were ever again equalled; but his successors, whatever their individual merits, transmitted the essentials of Pisanello's achievement. They represented men, with faithful realism, as individuals: they worked in a relief high enough to allow full significance of detail in the treatment of hair and eye and mouth—the most distinctive characteristics of every human face; they experimented incessantly with the relationship of a portrait to the space in which it was set; and they avoided, for the most part, all such decorative elements as did not come from the face or clothing of the portrait itself.

It is interesting, in this respect, to observe the influence of Italy upon neighbouring countries in which the production of medals for special occasions was also becoming a normal custom. Thus Giovanni Candida, of Naples, who combined a diplomatic career with the work of a medallic artist, was in Flanders in the service of the house of Burgundy in the 1470s and from 1483 at the court of France. His medal of

Antony, Bastard of Burgundy (89), shows much that is purely Italian in style and much (for example, in the heavier, fuller forms and in the stronger tendency towards elaborate decoration) that must be attributed to northern taste, which was to make the medals of Germany proper so much less pleasing in general than those of Italy and France. France was strongly affected by the Italian style. Medals made for Charles VII (1422–61) were still in the stiff Gothic idiom, struck in low relief without attempt at humanistic treatment of the king enthroned in majesty. But under Charles VIII (1483–98) the Renaissance style was beginning to touch French work, as is shown by the elegant medals (95) produced by Jean and Louis Lepère and Nicholas of Florence when the king and his queen, Anne of Brittany (96), made a state entry into Lyons in 1494. The city melted down gold to make a golden lion holding a cup containing a hundred gold medals: on these pieces (which were struck, and not cast) the king and queen were portrayed, still with something of that dispassionate, unhuman aloofness which characterizes Gothic work, and set against a field of lilies and ermines, exactly as early tapestries cover the field with flowers; but the treatment of hair and features shows that realistic portraiture, conceived in the Italian manner, was very near. It was achieved under Louis XII (91), to whom Anne was subsequently married, and with whom she made a second ceremonial entry into Lyons in 1500. Medals were again made; but this time cast portraits stand out in high relief and exhibit all the attention to feature and character, and all the appreciation of individual feeling, for which the Italian school had now for three-quarters of a century been famous.

Pisanello and his successors, by bringing to life in the medal that freedom, reality and rhythmic design which draughtsmen, painters and sculptors alike had all begun to enjoy so splendidly, could scarcely fail to influence the coinage of their times. Coinage, as has been seen, had languished—with brief and surprising exceptions—for many centuries in a sterile tradition of unrealistic and mainly linear design: it had become the product of simple engravers who for the most part lacked both the vision of the artist and the modelling technique of the sculptor. It was inevitable that fifteenth-century Italy should seek some means of transferring to coinage something of the new beauty of medallic art. There were, of course, differences to be considered and difficulties to be overcome. In particular, coins were struck from engraved dies, while Pisanello's medals were cast from moulds of which the models had been prepared in relief: the difference was between the technique of the metal-engraver and that of the sculptor-modeller—until, that is to say, coin-artists developed the technique of the puncheon, which could be carved *in relief*, in surpassingly hard metal, and which punched the main lay-out into the dies, which could then be finished off by engraving. Then again, the average size of coins, in Italy as elsewhere, was still appreciably smaller at this time than that of the average medal: Renaissance artists were well aware that a particular idiom of design is as successful in one size—the size in which it is originally conceived—as it is mysteriously unsuccessful in others; and consequently they made no attempt to transfer the idiom of medal design bodily to the coinage. Thirdly, while the relief of coins might in some cases be almost as high as that of medals, reasons of convenience increasingly dictated that it should normally be much lower, and therefore the artists who were anxious to impart a new "medallic" air to coinage had to bear in mind the differences which would be caused by the play of light on metal struck in low relief as opposed to the quieter and more subtle surface of metal cast in higher relief.

Nevertheless, the differences were accurately comprehended and the difficulties were overcome—not least because of the aesthetic and intellectual climate of a time which, as in classical Greece long before, demanded that coinage, however utilitarian its purpose, should wear as fine an appearance as contemporary artists could give it. Italian artists of the fifteenth century were often men of the widest and most impressive versatility, of whom such a man as Leonardo da

Vinci is only, perhaps, the best known: many of them were, at the same time, painters and sculptors and architects and metal-casters, and practised widely differing techniques with equal facility. Their services were accordingly in constant demand at the princely courts of Italy, whose rulers, papal or otherwise, at such places as Rome and Mantua and Ferrara and Milan, required the constant adornment of palaces, churches and towns with everything that could be achieved in painting, architecture, sculpture and metal-work. Some famous medallists, as we know, took the initiative in re-creating the coin-designer's art.

Cristoforo Foppa of Milan, surnamed Caradosso, was the son of a celebrated goldsmith, and himself achieved fame in the goldsmith's art. But he turned his attention to medals also and, with Benvenuto Cellini, paid particular attention to the substitution of mechanical for manual methods of coin-striking, heralding the end of a technique which had remained without essential change since the earliest Greek days. His most notable and magnificent work in coin-design was carried out in the latter part of the fifteenth century for the court of the Sforza family at Milan, whose coinage attained a perfection without parallel at the time. Although his Milanese dies were unsigned, it is possible to point to coins of so rare a delicacy in conception and so refined a perfection in execution that they must be attributed to his authorship. The portraits of the young Giangaleazzo Maria Sforza, the minor (94), and of his guardian and uncle Lodovico Sforza (93), who usurped the duchy of Milan in the last quarter of the fifteenth century until his capture by Louis XII of France in 1500, are works of superb quality in which, as has been rightly remarked, the representation is as light and delicate as if they had been formed in the medallist's wax and not by the tools of the engraver. Seldom can any artist have depicted with such unaffected certainty the contrast between almost virginal beauty, seen in Giangaleazzo, his youthful features unsullied, his hair falling in the elegant, lightly curled and lively fashion of the adolescent, and ruthless strength, as seen in the features of Lodovico, grimly set and uptilted below a formidable mass of stiffer, thicker hair.

A second eminent artist who left his mark on coinage-design was Francesco Francia of Bologna, renowned for his skill both as a painter and as a die-cutter (90) in the same period as Caradosso. His dies for the money of Giovanni II Bentivoglio, lord of Bologna from 1462 to 1506, are of a quality less refined, and an execution much less polished, than those which Caradosso was making for the Sforza. Nevertheless, they remain highly distinguished: Maximilian I, the head of the Holy Roman Empire, granted the right of coinage to the lords of Bologna in 1494, and the Bentivoglio family can have little regretted the strong, simple and dignified representation of Giovanni II which came from Francesco Francia's hand. He worked also for the Este of Ferrara and for the Sforza of Milan; and it is tempting to recognize his influence both in the portrait of Ercole I d'Este and also in that of Giangaleazzo Sforza (92)—the latter, in particular, remarkable for its light, fluid and admirably proportioned forms.

In the hands of such masters as these the essence of the new art of the cast medal was successfully translated, by the medium of engraving, to the struck coinage. In one respect the adaptation, so brilliantly achieved, was made easier. The medallists, on the whole, were required to devise two designs of equal merit for each medal—one for the obverse and one for the reverse. But the coin-designer had no need to worry, usually, beyond the execution of the obverse portrait: as the Sforza and Bentivoglio coins show, the reverses were often devoted to heraldic designs which, though they called for exactitude in balance and rendering, could be treated as formal patterns. Italian designers of the late fifteenth century thus propounded a formula for coinage-design which, with comparatively unimportant variations, has continued until the present day.

The influence of Renaissance Italy upon the designers of coinage elsewhere in Europe is of absorbing interest. In both

146

France and Germany, as has been seen, the new conceptions and techniques of the Italian medallists were beginning to be felt at the end of the fifteenth century. But France, in particular, was during that century enjoying a coinage of matchless Gothic splendour, in which the utmost elegance of design was combined with singular perfection in the engraving of dies. Therein lies one of the curious ironies of aesthetic history. The countries of northern and eastern Europe in general had not progressed, in their standard of coinage-design, beyond the uncouth conception and style of the darker ages surveyed in the last chapter; but in France— as in England and Spain, both strongly influenced by the traditions of French artists—the originally stiff Gothic style, with its love of the sharply rising point, of slenderness and of elaborate delicacy, was rising to a high degree of strength and slender grace. In France itself an astonishing change in monetary art took place with Louis IX (St. Louis) in the second half of the thirteenth century. The whole aspect of the coinage was revolutionized: not only were the dies suddenly executed in a conspicuously fine technique wholly at variance with that of previous reigns, but the artists produced designs which were memorable for their elegance, taste and balance. Under Philip IV (1285–1314) new beauties were achieved: the king was now represented in person, enthroned with sceptre and lis within a most graceful tracery of Gothic spandrels (100), while on the reverse the Cross which had for so long been the basic design of "unpictorial" medieval coinages was adorned, and its angles filled, in the finest of decorative Gothic styles (cf. 103–5). The high peak of Gothic florescence was reached under Philip VI (1328–50), whose gold coins were masterpieces alike of design and execution, showing the king enthroned against a noble architectural background of pointed arches and pinnacles, all richly crocketed (102), or within a sumptuously draped pavilion, its curtains drawn back to reveal the fleur-de-lis hangings within (101). Nor was Philip content with the decorative symbols of kingship alone. His gold "angels" provided what was undoubtedly one of the

147

outstanding coin-designs, outstandingly rendered, of the late
Middle Ages, and his gold florins representing St. George and
the dragon—a type probably chosen, as has been said, because
his English enemies had seemed for too long to monopolize
the favours of that saint—were remarkable for their vivid
and even half-realistic suggestion of medieval chivalry. The
same lively spirit of nobility characterizes the "franc à
cheval" of Jean le Bon (1350–64), where the king, fully
armed, is seen galloping into battle with his sword raised—
a design by which he set himself, quite literally, at the head
of France's orders of chivalry.

Resplendent these coins were, and of an ever-increasing
flexibility in technique. But the master-artists who engraved
the dies were unable—or unwilling—to take the final step.
The king was still shown as a ceremonial figure: his kingly
dignity was conveyed by the whole magnificent apparatus
of architectural detail, robes, regalia and attitude, and no
attempt had been made to suggest his personal quality, his
royal individuality, by means of realistic portraiture. When
Jean le Bon died Pisanello was not yet born; but half a
century after Pisanello's death his influence was acting
strongly upon the die-engravers of Louis XII, whose medals
have already been noted. The Naples coins of the end of his
reign (97) showed his portrait rendered in Renaissance style:
it is a little stiff, perhaps even a little uncouth, but for the
first time the die-engravers were able, so to speak, to make a
"close-up" study of a king of France, to model his actual
features, to dwell on such characteristics as hair and eye and
mouth, and to relate the trappings of crown and vestment
to the dominant element in the design—the monarch shown
as a man. At length the tendency towards an ever-increasing
decorative idiom had been arrested in favour of simplicity
and realism; and the pattern-designs required for the
reverses of these pieces show the designers to have been
concerned much more with aesthetic balance than with the
multiplied splendour of detail for its own sake. It is likely that
the change in style marks a change in technique also—from

EARLY RENAISSANCE PORTRAITS (I)

89 Antony, Bastard of Burgundy (Candida) (p. 142 f.),
90 Giovanni II Bentivoglio (Francesco Francia) (p. 146),
91 Louis XII of France (p. 143)

EARLY RENAISSANCE PORTRAITS (II)

$\frac{92}{93 \mid 94}$ 92 Giangaleazzo Maria Sforza (p. 146), 93 Lodovico Maria
Sforza (p. 145 f.), 94 Giangaleazzo Maria Sforza (p. 145)

dies wholly engraved to dies impressed by relief-puncheons and then finished off by engraving.

In Spain the naïve simplicity of the earlier Gothic style, seen in the attractively opposed portraits (98) of Ferdinand and Isabella (1474–1504), was not strengthened by naturally good technique on the part of the die-engravers, and (except for Spanish coinage in Italy and the Netherlands) the influence of the Renaissance portrait was to a large extent lost in the face of a growing love for elaborate heraldic designs. Elsewhere the most remarkable development in the art of coinage occurred in England. There the history of monetary art had, from the early medieval period, followed along lines closely similar to those of France. After the brief and splendid blossoming under Offa (above, p. 115 f.) Anglo-Saxon coins settled into a more or less stereotyped form. With virtually no exceptions they were silver pennies of a relatively small size which, though it had given encouragement enough to Offa's artists, failed to inspire their successors to real effort or experiment. For over four centuries the designs were chosen from a sadly restricted range—a stylized portrait, in no case truly modelled, never realistically conceived, and seldom engraved with any fineness of touch; or a cross, sometimes quite plain, sometimes decorated, with an inscription running round it. The Anglo-Saxon coinage was often full of a quaint and curious interest, but it failed to show among its whole range a single example in which real beauty of conception was matched by conspicuous excellence of technique. To some extent this was due—as the not dissimilar idiom of contemporary French coinage was likewise due—to the surprising decentralization of mints which prevailed. In any English town of consequence the local goldsmith would operate a mint under licence from the king; and, provided that he engraved dies of a pattern originally approved by the king, the quality of their workmanship was immaterial so long as the coinage was of good metal and full weight. Thus, in the several dozen mints scattered up and down the land, engravers felt it much less necessary to produce dies of high

quality than to conform, however crudely, to the prevailing
royal formula; and, when required to represent the king's
portrait helmeted or crowned or in armour, or to show his
full-length figure enthroned, they did so in a merely crude
and perfunctory fashion, as men who had never heard of
designs rendered in true relief and who could, indeed,
scarcely engrave even a simple linear design.

Nor did the Norman conquest bring any improvement.
Although the coin-designs were perhaps more boldly
engraved and although the coins themselves were perhaps
more efficiently struck from their dies, the standard of artistry
still remained coarse and simple. Yet a desire to achieve some
sort of variation must have been growing: the coins which
appeared under Henry I (1100–35), though they were in
general of the roughest quality, include certain examples on
which the engraver, greatly daring, attempted to represent
a three-quarter portrait (106) rather than the normal,
stylized profile or full face. The aesthetic value of such
experiment in an age of standardized forms is not to be under-
estimated, and, barbarous though the workmanship was, we
can at least share with these adventurous engravers the
excitement of seeing on the coinage what no man in that time
had ever seen. But for the anarchy of Stephen's reign
(1135–54) some further real improvement might have
taken place, for in York at least the die-engravers worked
their way towards a coinage which sometimes came near to
distinction and which, in its suddenly shown fondness for
pictorial conceptions suggesting action or mobility, is perhaps
reminiscent of the idiom of the contemporary German
bracteates (above, pp. 117 ff.)—not altogether surprising in view
of the part played by the Empress Matilda. It is not impossible that the naïvely charming designs of the baron Eustace
Fitzjohn (107), a supporter of the Empress, were engraved
under the influence of German models, for, although the
treatment of human and animal forms is simple to a degree,
the designs nevertheless show an interest in movement
which was entirely new to the English coinage.

But the long years of painful and costly war in which England attempted to dominate wide territories in France finally decided the traditions of English coin-design. For the French idiom exercised an irresistibly strong influence— the influence of a fashion and an elegance from which the English court and English artists could not remain immune. There was, moreover, a second factor of importance. Under the Anglo-Saxon and Norman kings English mints had numbered three dozen or more. But with Edward I they were reduced to about a dozen, and the effect of this was at once seen in a far more conscious and careful technique. The exciting and remarkable change in the aspect of French coins under St. Louis (above, p. 147) was now echoed by similar change under Edward I, who, on his newly introduced groat or fourpenny piece, imported the complete French style, with the king's formal and boyish facing image set within a graceful Gothic tressure. And by the time of Edward III (1327–77) the English coinage had attained the full splendour of the finest French work. It was from the French models, indeed, that the artists of Edward III at first borrowed their principal conceptions, rich in architectural detail and magnificently adorned with decorative detail. And probably the artists themselves were French, for the coins which Edward struck in France, either in his own name or in that of the Black Prince, were of the purest French conception and execution. Of these, two are specially noteworthy. The gold "guiennois" of Edward III (109) showed a full-length figure of the king, completely armed, standing beneath a Gothic portico with leopards lying on guard on either side. Here the richness of the formal vision is matched by the refined strength of the whole design in which, though the realism and the mobility of the Renaissance are wholly absent, the possibility of movement is so vividly suggested by the king's seemingly alert vigilance as he turns his head sharply to one side. Even more remarkable was the type of the gold "hardi" of the Black Prince (108), for this stands intermediate between the stiffly ornate Gothic presentation of kingship and the more fluid, individual and intimate idiom of large-scale Renaissance portraiture. The Black Prince faces us, a half-length figure, his hair and features as formal as the upward pointing finger on his breast. But already the treatment of the drapery is softening, and the artist's interest has been caught by the problem of representing its undulating folds in a realistic manner. Moreover, the master who designed this die, in an age when sumptuous decoration of all redundant space was the normal fashion, was content—and dared—to leave the field totally devoid of ornament within its encircling tressure. By this means he concentrated upon this larger and more personal portrait, so lifelike in its almost voluptuous forms, an emphasis which the Italian artists themselves were only just beginning to estimate and enjoy.

It was on the gold that English artists of this period lavished their greatest care: the silver bore designs which called for little imagination or genuine skill. But under Edward III the volume of coinage poured out in both metals greatly increased; and to this increase is probably due the growing practice of making dies from puncheons. There is little evidence that Greek and Roman dies were made otherwise than by the direct intaglio-engraving of metal; and the comparative poverty of most post-classical coinages down to the central medieval period suggests that dies continued to be thus engraved direct, by men who were normally unable to "model" what they hollowed out, or to do more than engrave in a purely linear style assisted by a number of simple punches. But the sudden improvement of French technique under St. Louis, and of English under Edward III, argues not only that artists of this time enjoyed a finer artistic vision but also that they were using finer instruments and methods. The gold "hardi" of the Black Prince is conspicuous for its combination of low relief and subtle modelling, and it is likely that in the middle of the fourteenth century the foremost coin-artists of France and England began to experiment with puncheons. A puncheon (in con-

THE RENAISSANCE IN FRANCE

95, 96 Charles VIII of France and Anne of Brittany (Jean
and Louis Lepère and Nicholas of Florence) (p. 143)

ITALY, FRANCE AND SPAIN: FIFTEENTH CENTURY

THE GOTHIC STYLE IN FRANCE

ARCHITECTURAL GOTHIC DESIGN

trast to a punch, bearing a single character or letter-stroke in relief) would bear the whole of a central design—everything contained within the inscription of a coin; and, since from the puncheon the die itself would be punched out intaglio, the design on the puncheon would appear in relief. Thus, just as Pisanello called forth the art of the Renaissance medal by wax models prepared in relief, so too the masters of French and English coin-design may have revived the beauties of coinage by a technique which allowed them, as well, to conceive in relief the designs that were ultimately to appear in relief on coins. In this way they would, in fact, work as relief-carvers, and not as engravers; and as relief-carvers they would estimate far more carefully and minutely the problems of modelling which coin-design presented.

Nevertheless, even though the coinage of Edward III was undoubtedly stimulated by the flush of French excellence, and though his artists may have witnessed the steady development of new techniques, the English coinage was to continue in the Gothic style, highly decorative and devoid of realism, for another century. It is true that new designs were conceived, appropriate to English policy and English life, like that of the noble—one of the most famous of its age—which showed the king, fully armed and still boyish, standing in a warship disproportionately tiny, its curving timbers riding upon rippling waves and the sharply angled rigging framing the king's majestic figure(102). In this fine conception the elaborate setting of architecture and tapestry is exchanged for the panoply of naval power, on which England's growing wealth was based: there is no reality and no true sense of proportion, although the talented artist who made this design infused it with a strikingly successful rhythm—the strong, upright figure in his tossing, rocking ship. Even under Henry VI the conventional designs remained undisturbed. His French coins were among the most graceful and admirable pieces of their day, as witness his gold *saluts* (99), with the Virgin Mary and the Archangel Gabriel leaning on the shields of France

159

and England (her robe falls below her shield, gently folded, in a touch both decorative and tender), while the sun shines above and a scroll, inscribed AVE, flutters between them. But his English artists were not encouraged, or inspired, to produce any new challenge to their powers of vision and technique.

It was Henry VII who brought about the revolution, half a century after Pisanello's death and at a time when Louis XII of France was infusing the French coinage too with Renaissance ideas. In 1494 Henry appointed the German Alexander of Brugsal as engraver at the Royal Mint, at a salary of £10 a year; and the impact of a new artist, familiar with the new tradition of realism and adept in the art of die-cutting, was immediately reflected in splendid new designs. Of these, one was a superb profile portrait of the king (115), of which it has rightly been said that, from the point of view of absolute realism, it was not only the first but one of the very finest ever achieved on English coinage. A nation which for centuries past had been accustomed to seeing its monarchs represented, fully facing, in the most conventional manner possible, and latterly indeed as boyish and unbearded figures wholly at variance with the truth (113), now saw its king as he really was—lean-featured, sharp-chinned, his aquiline nose rising to steeply arched eye-brows, a mane of hair falling naturally in fine waves from below his towering crown. Once more the miracle was achieved: instead of the stock portrait into which a man was free to read, if he would, the whole formula of kingship the artist's eye had seen the king himself and his hand represented the characteristics which made him a man. In doing so Alexander broke away from the decorative, space-filling idiom of former generations. Within its border of lettering Henry's portrait, its passions and feelings obvious but controlled, sits austerely within an empty field, and the most subtle and most powerful element in coin-design was safely re-established—the proportion between mass and empty space.

But Henry VII's coinage was nothing if not varied in its appeal. A new gold coin—the sovereign—of a princely size

160

justifying its name was now also first coined, and this must rank among the most superb of all English coins, showing Alexander's versatility in another style. The obverse (111) was traditional, and represented the king seated in a great throne, architecturally treated, though it is noticeable with what skill the engraver has succeeded in varying the low relief of this ample design. On the reverse, however, Tudor magnificence burst forth in a new form (112)—a great rose, fully open, framed by a delicate Gothic tressure, with the quartered arms of England and France nestling at its very heart. The superlative quality of this reverse arises from many elements. The design is highly decorative but, being circular in nature, is disciplined to the shape of the coin. The problems of relief in delineating a single emblem of so large a size are cunningly overcome by the treatment of the complex, curving and overlapping petals. The requirements of symbolism—now operative as a matter of course on English coin-reverses—are satisfied with perfection: the rose, the badge of the Tudor family, enshrines the royal arms. From all this there results a design in which we can admire true modelling, enjoy an astonishingly fluid complex of rippling form, and (by no means least important) comprehend with immediate insight and emotion the political symbolism which is conveyed.

The innovations made by Henry VII at the end of the fifteenth century cast the English coinage into a state of aesthetic flux from which it did not emerge, in a settled form, for a century to come; and that century of coinage is in many ways the most interesting and lovely in the whole English series. Convention and tradition vied with new idioms of presentation: Gothic decoration gave way slowly before the advance of Renaissance taste for larger designs more amply conceived and more spaciously set; and minting-technique was under constant examination, especially as the result of mechanical experiments being made in Italy, Germany and France. The reign of Henry VIII saw the gold angel transformed from a coin of clumsy conception and execution into a sophisticated and delicate design. Under Edward VI intense progress towards realism was made, the boy-king's bare-headed portrait (116) conveying all the simple, unemotional pathos of the finest coin-portraiture of any age. Mary Tudor, as we cannot doubt, employed some of the best artists of her day to engrave the noble portraits which characterize her coinage. And with Elizabeth, some of whose coins were struck, temporarily, by machinery, the artists achieved something which, never merely neat on the one hand, and yet always curiously decorative on the other, suggests that during her long reign they were consciously solving the problem of what, in the low relief of the time, made the perfectly designed and perfectly finished coin. That they were primarily concerned with proportion is clear enough in the light of such nobly economical designs as those of the gold pounds of 1565, where delicate modelling, splendid lettering, and ample spaciousness all play their part (117–18). But magnificence was never far away—magnificence of a new and more disciplined kind than had flashed out from the sovereigns of Henry VII; and some of the patterns (119) prepared by the queen's chief engravers at the Mint show what subtle splendours were exciting their artistic powers, and how strongly the imagination can run when it is freed from the paralysing weight of past traditions.

A century of experience and experiment in England had thus promoted coin-design from the late medieval phase of dies finely engraved in a heavily decorated linear style, devoid of portraiture, to one in which realism in portraiture was the principal element, contrived by subtle modelling in the extremely low relief which contemporary technique demanded, and emphasized by a severe reduction of decorative features. The change was a change from splendour to economy, from fulness to balance, from a love of rich pattern to a more sparing rhythm, with the interest in portraiture always paramount; and with these changes there came also a steady improvement in the technique of those who engraved the dies and struck the coins. English coinage in these hundred

ENGLAND: FROM NORMAN TO GOTHIC

106 Henry I (p. 152), 107 Eustace Fitzjohn under Stephen
(p. 152), 108 The Black Prince coining in France (p. 153 f.)

ENGLISH GOTHIC

109 Edward III coining in France (p. 153),
110 Edward III (p. 159)

years was as handsome as any in Europe outside Italy. In Spain, as has been seen, true advantage of portraiture was never taken: in France, after the invigorating artistic reforms of Louis XII, the coinage settled down in a stereotyped form from which only the advent of the baroque was to disturb it; and in Germany (below, p. 168) the peculiar development of the large-sized *thaler* coinages linked the art of coin-design much more closely with medallic art proper, of which the more western parts of Europe still had little knowledge.

Only in Scotland were there, otherwise, developments of special interest. There, the influence of English design must always, to some extent be felt; but it was from the European continent that Scotland derived the stronger influences which were to make her coinage in many respects so lovely. The groat of James IV (1488–1514), with its three-quarter portrait (114), just preceded the profile portrait of Henry VII of England. Technically the Scottish piece was inferior, for the artists plainly experienced great difficulty in the modelling of the three-quarter features; but the conception as a whole, rich in its inheritance of Italian and French beauty, and greatly strengthened by the inclusion of the shoulders, is truly masterly. Under his successor James V (*d.* 1552) the continental influences are continued and deepened: his gold bonnet-piece must be set down as an outstandingly successful example of kingly portraiture, rendered in an idiom wholly foreign to the coinage of England, and the pattern-reverses of many of his coins look straight to French models, which is hardly surprising since Etienne de Laune himself, one of the chief coin-designers of Henry II of France (*d.* 1559), was at one time preparing designs for the coinage of Scotland. Nor was the French influence likely to be diminished under Mary Queen of Scots, whose brief marriage to the Dauphin Francis took place in 1558. Her son, James VI, whose later coinage as James I of England was so singularly devoid of charm, struck a Scottish coinage which shows, by its contrast with the English, that good design is possible only when good designers are there to be encouraged. This memorable

165

Scottish series borrowed, unashamedly and enjoyably, from the best of what was being done abroad. From the high-ruffed shoulder-length portraits of Henry II of France came the inspiration for the young portrait (120) on his gold ducat: from the Italian medallists, surely, the extravagantly lovely conception of his gold "hat-piece" (122), the reverse of which, deliberately designed out of centre, again recalls the bold fantasy of Italian artists as the lion sits crowned, its sceptre held erect to a cloud in which appear the Hebrew letters for "Jehovah": from Italy again comes the spare, decorative grace of his gold twenty-pound piece (121), with motto inscribed on a quasi-medallic panel.

These compositions are all light and graceful in conception. In execution they fall short of the highest standards of their day, suggesting that the artists who drew the designs were not matched, in Scotland, by engravers of equal quality. Moreover, the actual technique of striking Scottish coins was inferior by comparison with the contemporary coins of England and France. The glory of Italian Renaissance work had been partly due to the fact that designer, engraver or modeller, and producer could all be, and often were, the same man. A century and a half after Pisanello's death the different functions were becoming detached and specialized. For a moment the advent of machinery—its introduction was even now imminent—seemed likely to restore a sense of unity between these functions; and attention must now be given to its effects.

CHAPTER VIII

Machinery and the Baroque

IF the European coinage of the sixteenth century showed the general extension, uneven and often strongly differentiated, of the ideas of the Italian Renaissance masters, that of the seventeenth century primarily reflected the influence of Germany. It has well been said that the medals of the German Renaissance introduce us to an atmosphere very different from that south of the Alps. In conception they were, from the first, much more massive, with an emphasis upon the heavy forms and the ornate, heavy clothing appropriate to the colder lands of the north and they seem to reflect the solid prosperity of the German mercantile classes. And in execution, too, they are stronger, bolder and less delicate; for German artists made little use of wax in modelling their designs, preferring to carve their models in wood or stone. The combination of these factors produced a series of medals which, though many of them are memorable (especially those attributed to Albrecht Dürer), are conspicuously deficient as a whole in the qualities of free imagination and fluid grace which characterize the Italian pieces. German artists tended to concentrate on a very large head in high-relief, in contrast to which the empty space around the head was meagre and the lettering often cramped and mean. Moreover, in designing their reverses they made plain their inability to work in imaginative pictorial forms, for these reverses were increasingly heraldic in nature, with coats of arms piled high in elaborate but essentially immobile effect.

Experiments with machinery for the striking of coins, to replace the age-old method of hand-striking by means of hammer-blows, had begun in Italy by the end of the fifteenth

167

century (above, pp. 142 ff.), and by the middle of the sixteenth machinery was so well advanced in Germany that Henri II of France bought, for 3000 crowns, apparatus which he installed in the Palace Gardens at Paris. The new mechanical methods had a remarkable effect upon the coinages of the astonishing variety of mints comprised within the Holy Roman Empire. For throughout the sixteenth century these mints increasingly adopted a new and large-sized coin known as the "thaler" from its being often made of the silver from the rich Joachimsthal mines. Although the relief of the designs upon *thalers* struck by machinery was naturally much lower than that of German cast medals, nevertheless the designs of the *thalers* were so elaborate, their portraiture was so strong and hard, and their diameter was so great that it is doubtful if they could have been efficiently produced by hand-striking. As it was, the introduction of the screw-press, which quite literally squeezed the coin-blank between the dies, enabled these large and thick silver coins to be minted without the loss of any detail in their complex designs; and thus the artistic features which were so noticeable in German Renaissance medals—full and heavy composition; large portrait-heads modelled in a rather harsh style; and intricacy of heraldic decoration—could be transmitted to the coinage and there turn into the baroque style, with exaggeration of selected features and weight of decorative detail taking the place of the simplicity and economy in which the Italian masters had excelled.

The *thalers*, large coins with a medallic pedigree, varied immensely in their design, and, in their different forms, exerted a stronger influence upon the coinages of Europe as a whole than anything since the Italian Renaissance itself, of which they were indeed a by-product. Some maintained the balanced sense of design, and the strong consciousness of the limitations of a circular field, which had been so striking a feature of the early German bracteates (above, p. 119 f). Thus the *thaler* of Archbishop Paris of Salzburg, coined in 1652, offers a composition in which the circular band of fine lettering in its inner beaded circle is deliberately broken at the top by the Archbishop's mitred head and at the bottom by the archiepiscopal arms. But more often the designers of *thalers* aimed at a more ponderous and more obviously powerful effect, and delighted in the representation of sturdy, bearded and armoured figures, as in the portrait—characteristic of so many others—of Johan-Georg I of Saxony (127), made in 1629. In this, by contrast with the Salzburg piece, the forms are harsh; and though the design was finely engraved on the die, and the coin itself admirably struck, the effect is one of over-elaboration. The field is filled too full, exactly as was the case with the earlier German Renaissance medals; and the artist, lovingly preoccupied with the minute particularities of the armour on the half-length bust, has reduced the portrait itself to an insignificant scale which is hardly superior to the conventional representations of the medieval Gothic style—of which it is the logical successor. In the course of another century German coin-designers had mastered the full magnificence of the baroque idiom. Granted the desire to adorn for the sake of adornment, they turned the decorative element to positive advantage in making their designs. The portrait of Joseph I of Hungary (129), made in the opening years of the eighteenth century for his double *thalers*, is a monument of extravagance. His features, indeed, are well modelled and present an excellently individual likeness, but the artist's main efforts have been concentrated on the monstrously large wig, which tumbles to either shoulder in a mass of curls far more elaborately rendered than any other single element in the design, and in a relief so high that they must almost have been undercut on the die.

Considered as a class, German *thalers* are more showy than beautiful, more magnificent than elegant. In conception they were large and splendid. In design they were heavy. In execution they were not seldom coarse. But their influence upon the coin-designers of other European countries was very great. Their size, in particular, recommended the adoption elsewhere of large coins—much larger, for example, than the

169

Italian *grosso* which the Sforza family portraits had so superbly adorned (above, p. 145 f.)—and on these large coins portraits of ample freedom, with maximum opportunity of modelling, could appear. Outside the Holy Roman Empire of Germany the standard of artistry was in general higher than in Germany itself. Not, perhaps, in those countries to which the baroque style came as the immediate successor to a style of pre-Renaissance crudeness. In Russia, for example, the influence of the German *thalers* led to a fine coinage, of large size, under Peter I (1689–1725), who introduced machinery to the mint of Moscow. Peter's portrait-bust (128) was in the manner recommended by the new German tradition—large and spread; strongly engraved but not modelled with delicacy; no more emphatic in the treatment of eye and moustached mouth than in the baroque rendering of falling curls and twisted drapery. In Poland, too, where the first *thalers* of Sigismund Augustus were of exquisite Renaissance grace, the style settled into the harsher, heavier forms dictated by neighbouring German mints. But elsewhere the freer, lighter forms of the Italian tradition prevailed more successfully.

French development of monetary art at this time was smooth and disciplined. Henri II, as we have seen, was quick to try the advantages of mechanical screw-press methods of coining imported from Germany. And although machinery was restricted, in 1585, to the coining of medals alone, leaving coins again to be hammered by hand, Nicholas Briot was once more perfecting machinery for striking coins in the early years of the seventeenth century; and from 1645 the manual method was obsolete. In combination with these developments the absorption by French designers of the essentials of the Italian tradition produced a coinage that was spacious, graceful, light and imaginative. Portraiture under Henri II, Charles IX, and Charles X, Cardinal de Bourbon, was extraordinarily effective—spare yet well proportioned; decorative but never ponderous. The first baroque features make themselves felt under Henri IV at the end of the sixteenth century: under Louis XIII, in the first half of the

170

seventeenth (130), they spring to full life, but with such superbly controlled sense of design at the hands of men like Briot and (even more) the great Jean Varin, and with such exquisite technique in die-engraving, that the new large-size French portrait-coins are masterpieces of orderly magnificence. Varin's portraiture, which was in its time to influence design in the England of Charles II just as strongly as the *émigré* Briot affected it under Charles I, was superb in its union of technical beauty, spacious conception and human feeling. This is perhaps most strongly felt in the soft and tender representation of the little Louis XIV at the time of his accession (133). The child is clad in the armour of a Roman general, and a victor's wreath encircles his brow, binding profuse, curling hair. But these baroque trappings detract in no slightest degree from the humanism of the portrait itself, with its rounded forms, its childishly undeveloped features, its suggestion of royal power and royal inexperience. Rather do they, by contrast, underline the true pathos of the portrait itself, which thus appears as the direct successor of the Italian realistic school merely coloured the more deeply, and presented more passionately, by the addition of these most unchildlike accessories.

Over sixty years later, when Louis XIV was an old man, his portrait-coins still showed him in all the baroque magnificence of mature middle age, his ample features thickened by the years but discreetly subordinated in aesthetic interest to the mass of sinuous curling hair that cascades to his shoulders. These later pieces of Louis, in both their portrait and reverse designs, show a superbly confident sense of ample and fluid form. Louis himself was a connoisseur of coins and medals. He amassed a royal cabinet which was the equal of any in the European palaces of his day, and the series of official medals which were struck in his long reign, although by their very numbers they tend to pall, were executed with unsurpassed polish and technique. The medals, indeed, followed a tradition in design somewhat different from that of the coinage. For while the coinage remained faithful to

171

large-sized baroque portraiture accompanied by elegant heraldic reverses, the medals were increasingly given over to neo-classical conceptions rich in allegorical figures and groups.

Elsewhere in Europe the decorative turbulence of the baroque idiom was variously transmuted or evaded. In Italy the most constant thread of monetary art was furnished by the Papal coins, and in these, with their ample and wonderfully impressive portraits (131), the lesson of the Italian Renaissance was seldom quite forgotten. The Papal coinage never failed to stress realism in portraiture as the designer's first duty. Moreover, the portrait—usually modelled with a skill and a subtlety not seen elsewhere—was almost invariably accommodated to the size of the coin with the fullest understanding of the rules of proportion. Indeed, the coins of *thaler* size issued by the Popes, especially in the seventeenth century, are a powerful reminder of the great superiority of the Italian idiom—light, mobile and graceful, however heavy the actual features to be portrayed—over the German, in which the massive weight of natural forms was deliberately accentuated in order to increase the effect. This is all the more remarkable, perhaps, in view of the powerful part taken in the design of seventeenth-century Papal coins and medals by the redoubtable family of the Hamerani, originally of Bavarian stock. But this phenomenal dynasty (which produced two woman engravers, one of them—Beatrice—of great repute) settled so firmly in Rome that the influence of northern idiom was evidently soon forgotten. Nor was Italy as a whole much affected by the baroque fashions in which the rest of Europe indulged. Humanism, naturalism and the love of grace in ornament were still the qualities demanded of an artist in designing coins; and, to illustrate the last of these qualities, one might point to the beautifully engraved and delicately conceived *thaler*-sized pieces of Cosimo III of Leghorn (1718), with a flowering rose-bush covering the field in a lightly balanced profusion (132).

The three centuries and more which, by the end of the

THE TUDOR SPLENDOUR

111, 112 Henry VII (p. 160 f.)

ENGLISH PORTRAITURE: EDWARD III TO
EDWARD VI

eighteenth century, had passed since Pisanello's death had thus witnessed a total revolution in the aspect of the coinages of Europe. A continent in which only simply designed and roughly executed coins of small size were prevalent at the close of the Middle Ages now furnished a range of monetary art which, though it varied greatly in quality from one region to another, was nevertheless as universal in its fundamental idiom as had been the art of the many city-states which covered Greece in the fourth century before Christ. From Russia in the east to Spain in the west coins were being designed in essentially the same tradition, with realistic portraiture as a standard requirement. The rediscovery of true portraiture, and indeed of the subtle qualities of the human form as a whole, was of course the paramount legacy of the Italian Renaissance masters, whose medals must always rank with the earliest sculptural coins of the Greeks for their sheer inventive power and for their swiftly acquired technical polish. It was inevitable that artists should, sooner or later, seek to reproduce the general aspect of Renaissance medals upon coinage also; and because the Italian genius of the time lay no less in the invention of machinery than in the creation of pure design, the requisite coining-machinery, enabling much larger quantities of much larger coins to be stamped from dies of steadily increasing elaboration, was already being tried out in Italy by the early fifteenth century. Mechanical methods, spreading swiftly to Germany, were in due course adopted by other countries, and here too its effect was seen in the increasing size of coins and the enlargement of the field available for the engraver's skill. All over Europe coins became more and more medallic in character. Portraits might be treated in a more or a less ornate fashion, and reverse-designs might be purely heraldic, purely decorative or purely animate in their conception; but all were alike in the amplitude which a large field encouraged and in the increasingly high relief which the new machinery allowed.

In contrast to the quasi-medallic transformation of coin-design under the influence of mechanized mints, the art of the medal, which suddenly sprang to full and perfect life in Pisanello's hands, suffered a steady decline. The peculiar excellence of the Renaissance medal lay in its being cast and not struck. But the growing perfection and power of machinery induced artists more and more to contemplate mechanical methods for the production of medals also. Thereby they endangered, and from time to time quite destroyed, the peculiar qualities of the medal. The art of the mechanically struck coin, invading the province of the medal, substituted for the high relief and skin-rough texture of the cast medal designs which were executed in lower relief and finished with all the hard polish of striking. Moreover, identical methods of production tended to foster identity of style and even identity of concept as between coin and medal. For, while any skilled modeller and bronze-caster can perfectly well set up in his own studio the modest apparatus necessary for the making of cast medals—the wax or clay model, the small furnace and the mould—the striking of medals could take place only where there was machinery. And machinery would exist only in the state-mints, so that medal-making in fact became increasingly the perquisite of the state, and less and less the opportunity of the individual artist to produce original design at the moment of his choice. The consequence in general was that, from the seventeenth century onwards, medals became official in tone, exactly as they were in the great series made in the reign of Louis XIV (above, p. 171); and although the artists responsible for designing them doubtless exercised a certain freedom in style and treatment, the idiom as a whole had to conform with that of the coinage itself.

Indeed, it is probably true to say that the large coins of *thaler* size which poured out from so many European mints in the seventeenth and eighteenth centuries temporarily killed the medal as an important and independent art-form, and that the relative oblivion to which medals are consigned even in our own day is partly the result of the application to them of a production-technique proper to coins alone. But, while the medals suffered, the coins undoubtedly gained advantage by borrowing from the medallist's art enough fluency in design, enough amplitude of field, enough height of relief, to transform them from the stiff and often stylized phase of late medieval design into pieces of extreme exuberance and frequently of great nobility. Europe in those centuries enjoyed a coinage of great variety. It was strong in inventiveness. Its designs, as a whole, were engraved with admirable skill and conceived along lines which were controlled by good taste. Above all there was desire for novelty. Medieval coinage could remain, century after century, without obvious change of design. But, granted the application of bold and realistic portraiture to coinage, its aspect and feeling were bound to vary, reign by reign; and although reverse-designs tended everywhere to take the form of heraldic patterns, sometimes very elaborate as in Germany, sometimes more spare and graceful as in France, it was nevertheless the case that artists cast about ceaselessly for any legitimate means of varying the presentation of the heraldic motif officially imposed upon them. They would have been dismayed at any such ordinance as the United States law of 1890, which laid it down that changes in design could not be made more often than once in every twenty-five years.

The tradition of coinage in England from the beginning of the seventeenth century was not dissimilar to that of Europe as a whole in certain of its main outlines. But it was by no means closely parallel. The full strength of Renaissance ideas in coin-design was not felt in England and Scotland until the very last years of the fifteenth century. And, although Renaissance design in Scotland developed fairly swiftly, as we have seen (above, p. 165 f.), its development in England was much more cautious and gradual. Tudor magnificence, as presented on the coins of Henry VII, Henry VIII and Edward VI (above, pp. 160 ff.), took a form unlike that of anything on the Continent. It was of its own kind, still obviously derived in many respects from the style of the late medieval money and yet exhibiting a decorative exuberance which owed much less to contemporary models across the Channel—

or even in Scotland—than it did to the inventive genius of English artists themselves. These artists were remarkably unaffected by the development of monetary art in Germany. Neither in the size of their coins nor in the style of their designs can we detect more than an occasional trace of borrowed foreign idiom. Even in the reign of Elizabeth I, long in years and splendid in the record of expansion, the insularity of English coin-design continued. All over the rest of Europe the use of machinery to supersede the immemorially old method of hammer-striking coins was being eagerly adopted, or at least tried out (as in France) for very considerable periods. But in England ten years sufficed for the Frenchman Eloi Mestrell before he was dismissed and his machinery thrown out. The cause of this resistance to mechanical methods (and of course to the much larger and thicker and higher-relief coins which they made possible) undoubtedly lay in the traditional and vested interests of the guild of moneyers within the now all-important Tower mint. Its result was to be seen in a coinage which, while that of Europe generally was moving steadily from Renaissance spareness to extravagance in form, showed by contrast a strong sense of discipline and even of austerity. The characteristic beauty of the Elizabethan coinage came from its spare balance combined with a tendency, specially noticeable at the end of the reign, to improve the technique of die-engraving to a point at which designs in extremely low relief could be rendered with the utmost fineness of detail.

In this last respect, indeed, the Elizabethan artists were reflecting, certainly and perhaps consciously, the current French style, flat, delicate and highly wrought. Its most famous exponent was Nicholas Briot (above, p. 170), who was not only an exquisitely sensitive and skilful engraver, but also something of a mechanical genius. His influence upon the artistic style of the French coinage was paramount from 1605 to 1625. From 1616 he was experimenting with machinery which would allow flatter, rounder and neater coins to be produced than anything which the hammer made possible;

178

ELIZABETHAN PORTRAITURE AND DESIGN

117, 118 Elizabeth I (p. 162)

ENGLISH AND SCOTTISH PORTRAITURE:
SIXTEENTH CENTURY

119 Elizabeth I (p. 162), 120–122 James VI of Scotland
(p. 165 f.)

and it is obvious that, unlike his great successor Jean Varin, he was not greatly interested in the opportunities which machinery afforded for striking high-relief coins from deeply engraved dies. When he left France in 1625 and moved to England he was to be one of a number of foreign influences upon English monetary and medallic art which, from that day onwards for two hundred years, blended English and continental traditions into a form that was nearly always interesting and often highly distinguished.

He came to England at a time when external stimulus was apparently much needed. The accession of James VI of Scotland as James I of England had resulted in a coinage of which it may be said without exaggeration that it showed no positive style at all. It was a mass of echoes and untidy borrowings from elsewhere: medieval motifs, brought up to date, stood side by side with the florid and now super-annuated splendour of Tudor forms, and the rich feeling for late medieval heraldic conception borrowed from Scotland was partnered by the first efforts at portraiture in a baroque style. But with the accession of Charles I in 1625 and Briot's removal to England in the same year an astonishing change came over the coinage—a change which was evident not so much in improved technique (though it was very greatly improved) as in the whole spirit of design. It is normally the sign of a master influence when an older set of conceptions is almost wholly abandoned in favour of new ones, when the aesthetic capabilities of a coinage are deliberately explored, and when, in addition to all this, new technical methods are developed in close association. And these were the fruits of Briot's activity in England.

His new machinery was at first confined to the striking of medals, and was not extended to coinage proper until 1629. But from 1628 he was busily employed in designing a variety of lovely portraits and equestrian figures which marked him out, under the protection and favour of a king who was him-self a connoisseur, as by far the finest engraver since Alexander of Brugsal nearly a century and a half before. The noble

essence of his style lay partly in the meticulously fine engraving of dies in extremely low relief (of which his famous
Angel is perhaps the most remarkable example): this was a
quality for which the coinage of France in his time had also
been conspicuous. But there was much more to Briot than the
ability to engrave so skilfully. His decorative instinct was seen
in an admirable taste, which at once delighted in all the
richness of scroll and curve, fold and curl, and yet disciplined
these ornaments severely to the requirements of a coin as a
whole. A design conceived and executed by Briot displays
perfection of form, freedom in composition, and balance of
proportion. The same design copied by a lesser contemporary
shows with what ease these elements could be coarsened and
confused.

Briot's silver coins of 1631–2, breathe the full spirit of his
excellence (123). The king's figure, mounted on a horse, is
modelled with the most extreme delicacy. Its proportions are
accurate: its isolation within the border of fine lettering is
nobly impressive; and its rhythm produces what is found
only in the best work, namely, a sense of movement which
appears easily to transcend the narrow confines of the coin.
On the reverse everything is decorative and bold. The
garnished shield ripples with ornament and, placed out of
centre as it deliberately is, sets up an opposition of balance
that is both exciting and satisfying. Much the same features
are to be found in the gold three-pound pieces (124) coined
out of requisitioned college plate at Oxford, to which, cut off
as it was by the encircling forces of Parliament, Briot as a
loyalist contrived to make stealthy and surreptitious visits.
Here the king's half-length bust is rendered in complete
magnificence, with crown and curls, lace collar falling over
his armour, sword and olive-branch. But here again is felt
that urgent sense of control, which has, so to speak, immobilized a moving and rhythmical view of the king for just
so much space of time as is necessary to see it on the coin.
The reverse of these noble coins is movement pure and simple:
by a conception unique in English monetary history a banner

floats, fold upon fold, across the field of the coin, proclaiming the king's adherence to the Protestant religion, the laws of England and the liberty of Parliament (125). It is doubtful if English designers have ever achieved anything more fluid or more original.

Few artists of his time in England could command the sum total of Briot's great qualities—perfection in engraving and rhythmical balance of composition. The latter quality, indeed, is something, springing from the heart and the mind's inner eye, which may not be teachable. But the former could be taught, and it is right to remark that, from the Stuart period onward, the coinage of England was produced from dies more finely and precisely engraved, perhaps, than any in the whole of Europe. The lesson of Briot's technical mastery was deeply absorbed and only forgotten with great difficulty. One at least of his immediate contemporaries came very near, if he did not in fact equal, Briot's skill as an engraver of dies. The Oxford crown (126) designed in 1644 by Thomas Rawlins was never struck or circulated in quantity, and the very rare surviving examples must therefore be regarded as patterns. But they show what a consummately fine artist Rawlins was, especially in the rendering of the king's horse, all fire and movement, with mane tossing and tail waving, against the placid view of Oxford city. Although the king's forms, by contrast, are weak and even clumsy, Rawlins's design must always stand out as one of the more heroic representations of English kingship, spirited and yet sublime in feeling, original in conception, and so exquisitely engraved that progressive enlargement only serves to bring out new beauties of detail.

Of the younger contemporary artists inspired by the perfection of Briot's style, and encouraged by constant mechanical improvements to explore the limits of that style, Thomas Simon was to become pre-eminent. In 1645 he was appointed head engraver at the mint, at first in joint tenure with another artist. But from 1648 onwards the direction of English coin-design was in his hands alone. It was ironical that, as soon as he attained this position, the royal patronage which had so brilliantly fostered Briot's genius was abruptly ended by the king's execution. The preceding chapters have called attention in many places to the extent to which coin-design was affected by the culture and taste of kings and rulers. Where the efforts of artists in general were harnessed to the cause of a régime, it seldom happened that the coinage was not adorned as part of a larger process. By contrast, when there were periods in which artistic achievement as a whole was denied encouragement or support in high places, the aesthetic standard of the coinage fell together with those of other artistic mediums. Now, with the death of the king in 1649, the puritan fanaticism of the Commonwealth turned violently against ornament as something that was, aesthetic-ally, almost sinful. Seldom can a change of mood have been reflected so clearly as by the coins which Simon was required to design—if indeed he did not leave them to his under-engravers—for the new powers. It was not just that they aimed at simplicity, with their plain English inscriptions "God with us" and "The Commonwealth of England" supplanting the Latinized name and titles and mottoes of a king. Far more significant was their total lack of rhythmic balance in design, which makes them among the ugliest and the most ill-conceived creations in the whole of the long English series.

But Simon was up against more than mere puritan Repub-licanism. Simple designs, unskilfully conceived, could be cut into dies by unskilful craftsmen, and hammer-struck by unskilful craftsmen to whom the new machinery, still not permanently installed, was a menace that might yet be resisted and driven out. If the moneyers thought along these lines, however, they were too late. Varin's improved machinery in France made French hammer-struck coinage obsolete from 1645. In 1649 the Commonwealth Govern-ment, keenly interested in economy and the avoidance of wasted effort, invited Peter Blondeau, engineer of the Paris mint, to instal new machines in London. Prejudice against Blondeau himself as a foreigner greatly limited his activity;

BRIOT AND HIS SCHOOL IN ENGLAND

123 Charles I (Briot) (p. 182), 124, 125 Charles I
(? Briot) (p. 182 f.), 126 Charles I (Rawlins) (p. 183)

GERMAN THALERS AND THEIR INFLUENCE

127 Johan-Georg I of Saxony (p. 169), 128 Peter I of Russia (p. 170), 129 Joseph I of Hungary (p. 169), 130 Louis XIII of France (p. 170 f.)

but at least the new machinery enabled Simon to produce, in 1656, a superb series of portrait-coins of Cromwell as Protector. Although, in the end, these were never circulated, they remain a supreme example of English monetary art (134). Low relief is combined with wonderfully sensitive modelling: engraving is of the finest and most delicate: the lettering is of classic strength and simplicity; and the use of ornament shows the utmost taste in its splendid economy. How much better to discipline abundance in design than to banish, as the standard Commonwealth coinage banished, even the very thought of aesthetic complexity!

This Cromwell portrait-coinage should probably be recognized as the high peak of English monetary design. Such indeed was the significant verdict of a French critic writing three-quarters of a century ago. For Simon's designs show an immense advance from the style of Briot, which, by contrast with the Englishman's ampler naturalism, seems to be almost precise and mannered. And yet Simon avoided the dangers of the baroque. It is true that he represented Cromwell with a laurel wreath around his head, and with his shoulders draped in classical style. But these elements are introduced softly, gently: their purpose—partly decorative, partly symbolical—detracts in no slightest degree from the primary purpose of the artist in creating the complete humanity of a fully naturalistic portrait. It is enough to compare this masterpiece with the splendid French creations under the young Louis XIV (above, p. 171) to appreciate the achievement of Simon in evolving a style which, though it naturally owed much to continental beginnings, was worked out along strongly individual and purely English lines.

Nevertheless, the Continent was to defeat him under Charles II, assisted by the difficulties in his own nature, which resulted in a flow of dies from his workshop much slower than a newly mechanized mint demanded. In 1661 Jan Roettiers, an Antwerp artist, was called over to act as joint head-engraver by Charles, who had been assisted during his exile abroad by Roettiers' father. Since the two men could not work together a trial of skill was ordered, for which Simon designed his famous Petition crown in 1663. The fact that the king felt obliged, on personal grounds, to prefer the highly competent though plain and uninspired work of Roettiers to that of Simon need not blind us to the splendour of Simon's creation. He represented the king full-busted (*Frontispiece*) and in a scale larger than that used for the Cromwell portrait. The relief, too, is considerably higher, and the exuberance of detail much more marked: the hair cascades in waves which, while they are not extravagant, are remarkably soft and fine in their rendering and extend around the neck on to the far shoulder. In these respects Simon was conceding to the increasingly baroque tendencies growing up abroad. But his concessions fell far short of imitation. Just as in the more subtle and disciplined Cromwell portrait the portraiture itself took precedence of all other adjuncts, so too in the Petition crown the delineation of the king's features— immeasurably superior to what Roettiers could contrive— concentrates the observer's full and avid attention upon a feat of modelling and characterization for which no praise can be too high.

On the edge of this lovely piece appears an inscription stamped in tiny letters: "Thomas Simon most humbly prays your Majesty to compare this his tryall piece with the Dutch and if more truly drawn & emboss'd more gracefully order'd and more accurately engraven to releive him." In fact he was not relieved of his office, but the most important work henceforth was put in the hands of Roettiers, who was soon joined at the Mint by his brothers Joseph and Phillip, and, when these subsequently left England, by his own sons James and Norbert. The achievement of the Dutch school of artists in England down to the end of the seventeenth century remained competent: in particular the standard of engraving continued on that high level—so much higher than in the majority of continental mints—which Briot and Simon had established. But in conception their coins were undistinguished; and, even when the artistic direction of the

Mint came under English influence again with Croker and Yeo and Tanner in the eighteenth century, it seemed as if the moment of impulse had somehow been lost. Pattern pieces of most unusual elegance and taste prepared under Anne (135) show what might have happened to the coinage of that early Augustan age if continental idiom had been abandoned in time. And the earlier coinage of George III, especially the large coppers of the last decade of the eighteenth century, demonstrate once more the peculiarly English fondness for ideally delicate execution. But it was not until the association, later in his reign, of William Wyon with the Italian Benedetto Pistrucci that a new departure in English coinage took place, which was to lift it up and away from the semi-classical baroque style. And the products of this new idiom belong to another chapter.

Meanwhile there had arisen, in America, another great group of coinage of European origins. By the middle of the sixteenth century the whole of central and south America was in the effective or nominal possession of Spain and Portugal; and in these great regions the tradition of Iberian coinage, with its emphasis on heraldic designs to the exclusion of portraiture, generally prevailed. In the north American continent the development of design followed along very different lines. Of the earliest New England coins those of Massachusetts, made in 1652, reflected with extraordinary fidelity the plain and austere aesthetic climate of contemporary Commonwealth England, and are far more curious than attractive. Not until the reign of George I was anything like a universally available colonial coinage produced for the American colonists. It was designed by an Englishman, William Wood, and the king's portrait was accompanied by the not ungraceful "Rosa Americana" type, symbolizing the transplantation of English culture to the New World. The collapse of English power in the face of American resistance under George III led to a great variety of coins from the different rebellious states. But few of these showed even the slightest aesthetic sense. Only when a "United States"

189

coinage proper was instituted in the last decade of the eighteenth century was any very serious attention given to questions of design. The House of Representatives favoured a figure symbolical of Liberty as the chief motif of the new coinage; and the Senate ultimately agreed. Not unnaturally the revolutionary movement in France strongly affected the imagination of the Swiss artist Droz who designed the head of Liberty (136), bearing a classical cap of freedom on a pole across her shoulder. This conception, although it was not engraved in any specially fine technique, nevertheless compels attention as a deeply felt, spirited and excellently proportioned device.

America absorbed her aesthetic theory—or all that her early citizens had time for—in a ready-made form imported from Europe. Europe herself was at the same time completing an artistic process in coin-design which had begun to stir in the thirteenth century and was in full vigour by the fifteenth. Artistic maturity, on a continental or even a regional scale, is not reached quickly. It is one jewel of the intellectual crown which is won, slowly and steadily, when peoples emerge from a long-continued state of confusion and flux and, rich in confidence and spirit, order their affairs with enjoyment and pride. The multiplication of coinage-issues in the seventeenth and eighteenth centuries all over Europe gave artists wide opportunity for the creation of new conceptions and styles. More important, the growing perfection of machinery turned their attention increasingly to questions of technique. The singular quality of such men as Briot and Varin and Simon lay in their ability to exploit machinery without surrendering anything of their rich creative powers. In this they set a challenge to all their successors—a challenge which the ultimate perfection of machinery in the later nineteenth century made it especially difficult to meet.

PORTRAITURE AND DESIGN IN ITALY AT
THE END OF THE SIXTEENTH CENTURY

131
132

131 Pope Innocent XII (G. Hamerani) (p. 172),
132 Cosimo III of Leghorn (p. 172)

EUROPE AND AMERICA: THE SEVENTEENTH
AND EIGHTEENTH CENTURIES

133 Louis XIV of France (Varin) (p. 171), 134 Oliver
Cromwell of England (Simon) (p. 187), 135 Anne of
England (p. 189), 136 United States of America
(Droz) (p. 190)

CHAPTER IX

Machinery and the Modern Formula

A
T the beginning of the nineteenth century a remarkable change swept over the coinages of Europe. For a hundred and fifty years previously coin-designers had shown a love, sometimes passionate and nearly always emphatic, for elaborate decoration rendered in the baroque style, in conformity with the idiom of poets and painters and sculptors of the same period. Quite suddenly the elaboration dropped away. Where there had been ornament there was now plainness. Accumulation of detail gave way to something nearer simplicity. Portraits, instead of emphasizing the temporal part magnificently played by kings and princes, began to concentrate on their personalities. Character was felt to be of more importance than the ornate setting of robes and armour. The form of a man's own hair was preferred to the towering splendour of a peruke. In short, man himself was again the focus of interest. He might be treated in a romantic fashion; or his individuality could be suggested by an unromantic aloofness. But everywhere there was a movement away from complex artificiality. The French Revolution left its mark on infinitely more than the political institutions of France herself. To read Wordsworth after Pope is to appreciate fully the immensity of the change in spirit.

In France, indeed, the transformation in monetary style was complete. The extravagant portraits of Louis XVI—so unnaturally exuberant as to have become in a sense stylized —were succeeded by representations of Napoleon as First Consul which showed him in full classical simplicity (137). The designer of these splendid portraits was Nicolas-Pierre

Tiolier, destined to become chief engraver at the Paris Mint. He imparted to Napoleon's features certain qualities which enormously influenced his contemporaries. The political philosophy of the times, with its sidelong glances at the pristine virtues of Republican Rome, recommended classical forms. Napoleon's portrait was cut off at the neck in what is known technically as a couped bust: once more, after an interval of seventeen hundred years, the observer's eye is elevated, above the gently curving lines of the neck-truncattion, to the unadorned power of the features above. The hair lies in artlessly arranged locks—as it might be for another Augustus, due to establish another great empire. Eye and mouth are delineated with the utmost care and strength; and the compelling interest of the portrait as a whole springs, exactly as it had sprung in Greek and earlier Roman times, from the acute observation of these all-important features, passionately felt and rendered, invested with all the power of isolation. And the natural beauty of the conception is enhanced by the artist's consummate skill in proportioning the head—much larger than had hitherto been normal—to the size of the field.

Tiolier's classical idiom did not, and probably could not, last. It was the fruit of a short-lived mood of stern political inspiration, when the romance of revolution was giving way to a conscious desire for new leadership. His later work, culminating in the portraits of Louis-Philippe, shows a constant movement away from the sheer and fine simplicity of the Napoleonic likeness. But it never sacrificed two of its principal qualities: his heads continued to be so large that they could be modelled in admirable detail, and they continued also to represent men as men, with a full realization that only if eye and mouth are allowed to tell their story can a portrait possess its vivid and proper realism.

Much the same characteristics are to be seen—though perhaps in a rather more conscious and even archaistic form— in the portraits of Louis Napoleon, King of Holland, by the French artist George (139), and of Bernadotte as Charles XIV of Sweden in Borg's time (138). The former were executed between 1806 and 1810, and show mannerisms (for example, in the rendering of over-long hair and in the half-profile, half-facing eye) which bespeak a preoccupation with pre-classical rather than with merely classical idiom. The latter were made twenty-five years later, at a time when kings were beginning to appear as ordinary men. Bernadotte is shown in a stiffly ornate archaic style which seeks in no way to lessen (but rather exaggerates) the natural peculiarity of his features. Each, however, is a splendid achievement, in which admirable technique has been combined with an essential understanding of truly humanistic portraiture. And with them might be associated the work of Christian Teichmann for the principality of Nassau from about 1810 to 1815—splendid in conception and proportion, powerfully simple in presentation, and with the same concentrated brilliance of characterization that had marked the days both of imperial Rome and of the Renaissance.

A comparable movement away from the ponderous splendour of baroque ornament towards the character-portrait based on the classical tradition was made in England, where the history of nineteenth-century coin-design followed an interesting course. From the earliest years of the century it was guided, except for the intrusion of a single foreign artist, brilliant and wayward, by the members of one family of outstandingly good English engravers—the Wyons, of whom the two Thomas Wyons, father and son, were transferred to the Royal Mint from Matthew Boulton's commercial Birmingham mint in 1811, to be joined by William Wyon, a cousin, in 1816. At this same time Benedetto Pistrucci, an Italian and an exquisite carver of gems and cameos, was also associated with the designing of dies for the Royal Mint. The aesthetic partnership, though not personally happy, was a profitable one. The Wyons, who were indeed no mean artists (and William was a great one), excelled in their understanding of the technical processes of engraving dies and striking coins. Pistrucci, as a gem-carver, at first lacked the knowledge of monetary technique, but his inventiveness and his sense of proportion in design made him conspicuous among all his contemporaries. His best dies are probably those made for the crowns of George III in 1818. The king's head (140) was cut short at the neck according to the new idiom, and could consequently be shown in a large size which gave full opportunity for the most subtle modelling and the greatest delicacy in engraving even though the relief was extraordinarily low. Characterization is powerfully applied: the king's personality broods amply in this noble portrait, in which the treatment of the heavy eye and sensuously twisted lips contrasts with the easy classical grace of his curling hair. Pistrucci's reverse-design (141) was, if anything, even more remarkable, for here he abandoned outright the whole of the past tradition of the English coinage. Previous crowns had shown either a king's equestrian figure or a heraldic device of arms; but instead of such things we see a motif borrowed from Italian coins of a much earlier period and applied with complete appropriateness to English coinage—St. George slaying the dragon, surrounded by the Garter bearing its motto "Honi soit qui mal y pense." This composition is, in fact, a reversion to complete classical idiom, and, with its naked Greek-armed horseman mounted on a Parthenon-style horse, breathes the whole essence of the classical revivalism of the times. But, revivalist though it is, it stands out as one of the noblest innovations in English coin-design from 1800 to the present day, and it is not surprising that it has continued to be the reverse of gold sovereigns ever since.

The Wyons worked in a tradition that was less distinguished, gentler and (142) even romantic. The family's output of dies under Queen Victoria was phenomenal, not only for coins but for medals as well; and a constant preoccupation with medal-dies, rich in figured and heraldic detail, undoubtedly went far to confuse the essential distinctions between the technique of medal-design and that of coin-design (see below, p. 205). As a result the idiom of the coin-design probably

suffered: nevertheless some dies of splendid quality, were produced, notably for L. C. Wyon's 1860 "bun" penny (144, 146),
with as graceful and elegantly proportioned a portrait as could
be wished for, showing what was so rare at the time—a bust
not "cut" at the neck but with the shoulder-line extending
downward to the coin's border. In general, however, art was
already tending to become academic and eclectic, as it had
been indeed with Pistrucci's classical St. George also. William
Wyon was equally at home with the richly classical allegorical
figures which bedizened so many of his medals and with the
revived Gothic style of mid-Victorian years, so beautifully
employed for the patterns he made for the 1846 crowns (145)
—indifferent in portraiture but splendid in detail, balance
and proportion. The imagination of the coin-designer no
longer strove to conceive what was new. His eyes had begun
to search the past for what could be adapted. And what was
true of England was true of other countries in the European
tradition. The magnificent dies designed by Christian Gobrecht
for United States dollars in 1836 drew heavily upon classical
traditions (143): neither the free impulses of Republicanism
nor the natural vitality of a young nation resulted in any
strong desire for originality in conception. Republicanism,
indeed, has all too often robbed coinage of what should be its
principal interest in modern times—namely, portraiture. For
the substitution of the head of some abstract personification,
Liberty or Fertility or Youth or Labour, presents problems
which the sophisticated mind of the modern artist can face
only with great difficulty. The Greek artist, portraying the
imaginary head of some god or goddess, could easily infuse
it (in the earlier days at least) with the sense of personal
feeling or passion. But the pale spirit of national character in the
symbolical figures of the nineteenth and twentieth centuries
seems, by contrast, uninspiring and uninspired, for the very good
reason that we do not worship them, physically and emotionally, as the Greek worshipped the godlike creatures of his
own imagination. Only in the young republic of Eire has
the problem of symbolical design been solved, in western

terms, with any success. There Percy Metcalfe's fluid and easy forms are seen to fine advantage in his acutely observed and cleverly proportioned studies of horses and fish and fowl, which, if only the quality of the metal had allowed, would have attracted much more attention than the curiously little they have in fact received. Elsewhere republican symbolism has become either frigid and stiff or morally didactic except where the portraiture of statesmen past and present is from time to time attempted.

Interruption in the spontaneous flow of fresh conceptions during the last century is not, however, entirely the result of inability to invent. Artists, in whatever medium, have always been able to draw upon an imagination more highly charged and more strongly creative than those of their fellow-men; and if the products of this imagination are not always called forth the reason sometimes is that no conscious desire for them is expressed. In the preceding pages enough has been said to suggest the gradual development by which the originality and inventiveness of coin-designers came to be controlled by governmental agency. It is a far cry from Greece, where the astonishing fluctuations in the treatment of a given theme suggest very considerable freedom on the part of a designer, to the system of controls and committees and precedents and policies by which a modern mint, conducted as a government department, can subordinate its artists. Mints today are technical factories, run as businesses. Formerly they were not so much factories as workshops; and the artists whose influence dominated those workshops were themselves dominated by the influence of powerful patrons —kings or noblemen—whose likes or dislikes were usually an effective obstacle to any temptation of continuing old design, and avoiding the new, out of spiritual stagnation. It would be false, of course, to suppose that in former ages the new was always given an automatic welcome. For long periods, indeed—and the Byzantine empire furnishes an excellent example, novelty was frowned on, and traditional designs came to assert an unbreakable supremacy. Nevertheless design was, until lately, relatively free from mechanical conditions. A man copying traditional design had to do so by hand; and any man copying anything by hand is apt to introduce some subjectively felt innovation even into the most carefully prescribed pattern, since no two artists see the same thing exactly alike. But, with the transformation of artists' workshops into state-run factories and with the growth of policies of economy, it is easy to see that machinery may be used in a dozen ways to perpetuate the form of that which, if copied by hand, would have shown subtle differentiation leading, in time, to genuinely important advance.

Mechanism for the actual striking of coins was, as we have seen (above, p. 144), the first to be devised—through the ingenuity of Renaissance artists. This enabled a given pair of hand-engraved dies to strike more coins more quickly and more surely than could be done by manual labour. When the habit grew up of carving master-puncheons in relief, from which intaglio dies could be punched out mechanically, machinery was adding the quick multiplication of dies to its previously granted benefit of the quick multiplication of coins, and thereby increased yet more the multiplication of coins. The fundamentally important stage in the development of machinery was reached early in the nineteenth century by the introduction of the reducing-machine, first in France and subsequently, through the support of Pistrucci, in England. This machine increased the multiplication of master-puncheon for multiplied dies to a point at which a given design, once committed to coinage, is reproduced over and over again, in any required size, at extremely low cost—a circumstance which any government department, rightly cautious in the spending of public money, will consider at least as important as the encouragement of new design for its own sake.

To ponder over the coin-design of 2,500 years, leisurely and with an open mind: to compare much that is already familiar with what is unfamiliar or little observed: to banish all prejudice in the search for fine design—to do this is to

199

learn an immense amount. In particular it becomes quite evident that, from the time when the reducing-machine was first elaborated, the general standard of coin-design has almost everywhere declined. Use of the machine began in England in 1824. In the eighteen-fifties it was improved; and in the earliest years of the nineteenth century it was improved again. Its principle is simple. The artist forms his design in relief, in clay or wax, in a size very much larger than that of the intended dies. By this means he is able, if he wishes, to give to his large, sculptured model all the care which a Pisanello likewise gave to his models. He is, of course, aware, as the model takes shape under his hands, that much of what he does may ultimately be invisible, for the detail of the model—which may be as much as twelve inches across—must be reduced to a size no more than an inch and a half at the most. Aware of the changes which reduction is bound to cause, the artist will use a reducing glass in an effort to foresee them; and, when his model is finished—a model from which the Renaissance artist would have created cast medals in the same size—he then allows the reducing-machine to transform it into a variety of miniature sizes suitable for any current coin-denomination. From these small reproductions, which the machine cuts out, automatically, in steel, intaglio dies can thereafter be reproduced in perpetuity, sufficient in number to strike the vast quantities of coin required annually from a modern mint.

The process is economical: the machine breeds dies in large numbers at very little cost, and a single portrait-model can be used impartially for coins of all sizes in a current range. But the artist's work is produced at a double remove from what he made originally with his own hands. He models in relief, and in large scale: the mechanically reproduced die is intaglio, and of coin-size. Hence arise the more obvious of the defects caused by the employment of the reducing-machine. In the art of coinage the reproduction of the portrait, delicately modelled yet sharply impressed, is the most exacting test of quality of method. Yet modern coinage,

NINETEENTH-CENTURY EUROPEAN PORTRAITURE

$\frac{137}{138}$
$\overline{139}$

137 Napoleon as First Consul (Tiolier) (p. 193 f.), 138 Charles XIV (Bernadotte) of Sweden (p. 194 f.), 139 Louis Napoleon of Holland (George) (p. 194)

NINETEENTH-CENTURY ENGLISH PORTRAITURE

140

141

142

140, 141 George III (Pistrucci) (p. 196), 142 George IV
(W. Wyon) (p. 196)

however neatly produced, seldom achieves incisiveness of line in portraiture. The contours are fogged, however, infinitesimally: the impression is slightly soft: the definition—by contrast with coins struck from directly made dies—is quite certainly impaired. Thus the peculiar distinction of coin-design, namely, its fineness of clear line—a distinction for which the master-artists of all ages were famous, is lost.

This, however, is not the only loss caused by the extensive development of reducing machinery. More serious is the fact, as has been remarked by an eminent scholar, that its use removes the artist too far from the coin as a finished product. He designs the model, and may work upon it with loving care; but the processed die is not his, and he did not make it. The position has been put more strongly by the late Sir George Hill, who combined with his profound knowledge of technique an admirably subtle and catholic taste in aesthetic matters. He pointed out (what others since have also held) that no design can be reduced in size without endangering its internal relationships and proportions. "Neither modelling nor design can be truly translated on to a smaller scale except by an intelligent hand," he wrote; and a reduction "is about as true to model as a cheap colour-process illustration is to the original picture." Comparison of an artist's large-scale portrait model with the small-scale coins which are ultimately descended from it leaves no doubt that this judgement is essentially correct. Mint-engravers may re-touch the dies which are made, intermediately, in the reduction-process, deepening a shadow here and sharpening a detail there. But this is technical skill at second hand, and not artistry at first hand; and coins produced by such a process can scarcely be expected to show fine and elegant quality in line and mass. The current portrait of Queen Elizabeth II by Mary Gillick —a delightful conception, traditional in its origins but refreshingly novel in its detailed interpretation—is a legitimate example of mechanically produced coarsening (147). What was delicately modelled and cunningly built up, plane by plane and mass upon mass, is, quite literally, reduced to something in which definition is weak and the clear inter-relation of the parts is invisible.

Apart from considerations of economy there are, of course, arguments which can be brought forward in favour of the reducing-machine. There have been periods when a country's tradition of coin-design has lain narrowly confined, and some-times too narrowly, within the hands of a particular school of artists, resulting in stale conceptions and stereotyped forms. Use of the machine, it is claimed, brings into contact with monetary design those artists who have never learned to work in miniature, still less to cut dies intaglio. This is an argument of importance, for there is no doubt, as first the Greek record and then the Italian Renaissance showed, that fine coins are often the product of artists in another medium turning their attention to the special problems and technique of coin-design. And it is true that the modern custom, prevalent in many countries, of encouraging artists to compete for the designing of new coins is an admirable one. But it is also true that no work of art can be "finished" except in its final size. Those with whom the choice of coin-design in any country lies would powerfully serve the cause of monetary art if they required potential designers to model in the actual size of the coins to be designed. This would not mean that a model, once approved, could not be mechanically reproduced in the form of dies thereafter. What would be avoided, and most profitably avoided, would be the approval of a model which, when not only reproduced but also greatly reduced in size, runs a serious risk of sacrificing so many of the finer points that, in combination, distinguish great work from what is markedly inferior. Such a system would, indeed, call for as many master portrait-models as there are coin-denominations—nine in the case of England—instead of the single model which the machine arbitrarily adapts to any size. But would this be too great a price to pay for a quality which would approach so much more nearly to the indis-putable artistry of earlier times? The use of machinery in the production of the immense masses of modern coinage .

is inevitably necessary, and it can give to coinage what it had already begun to give in the seventeenth century, namely, a regularity of outline and an evenly applied impression. But its uncritical and uncontrolled use cannot be indulged in without essential harm to the artist's function in design.

The art of the medal, too, has suffered in the past by mechanical methods of production. Cast by the greatest Italian masters, as we have seen (above, p. 136 f.), medals had previously been hand-struck; and, after the Italian invention of screw-presses for coinage, machinery was in due course used for the striking of medals also. From the seventeenth century down to the twentieth the vast majority of medals in all countries were struck and not cast. What was sacrificed in the process is difficult to estimate. The subject-matter of medallic design tended everywhere to lose the charm and fancy of individual choice, for medals could only be struck where there was massive machinery, and this machinery could only be found in official mints where official ideas prevailed. Even more important was the sacrifice of those special qualities which cast Renaissance medals had so brilliantly displayed. A struck medal shows the surface of the metal uniformly hard in compression. The play of light over its ample field and high relief is relentlessly bright. The contours of the human portrait shine with a dominating gleam of metal which is wholly alien to the light-absorbing skin and hair of the living subject. By contrast a cast medal possesses a soft surface. Its interplay of light and shade is subtle; and the differing texture of skin and hair and clothing, which every modeller does his best to suggest in his sensitive plastic model, is faithfully reproduced in the surface of the cast metal.

A combination of these two prevalent defects—the increasingly official and impersonal nature of medallic subjects and the insensitive, unsubtle finish of struck medals, often turned out in over-abundance—has led to a remarkable decline in the interest and quality of medallic art in past generations. Louis XIV, as was noted, encouraged the striking of a great series of medals commemorating the events of his long reign; and few subsequent rulers omitted to produce similar pieces or to favour the making of semi-official medals on the same lines. Larger in size than coinage proper, higher in relief, and bearing specially chosen designs, these medals were nevertheless struck as coins were struck, and in their artistic essentials were no more than outsize coins, hard and shining and lacking the softness of surface required to do justice to their normally admirable and specially contrived modelling. Moreover—and this is an important point— nearly all struck medals made in the last hundred years have been through the reducing-machine first, and all the defects which must be assigned to coin-design when drastically reduced from the size and proportion of an original model must be similarly expected when medal-design is likewise reduced.

Fortunately modern medallists are becoming more aware of the dangers which threaten the quality of struck medals. In some cases great care has been taken to render the surface of the dies in such a way as to avoid harsh brilliance, either by delicately curving the planes of relief or by giving them a roughened texture which enables the medal's high relief to hold and not reflect the light. An exquisite example of this careful technique is to be seen in the portrait-medal of Toulouse-Lautrec by André Galtié of France—a country which can claim also in Henry Dropsy one of the greater medallists of the age. But Dropsy, like the equally dis- tinguished Theodore Spicer-Simson of America, has always preferred the cast technique, by means of which, without loss of definition, their designs have attained that combination of delicacy and depth and variety which must always be the object of a sculptor working two-dimensionally in an artificially limited field. And in the years following the second world war the cast technique has continued to gain ground, especially on the continent of Europe, where feeling for free design, away from traditional formulas, has also been conspicuous,

NINETEENTH-CENTURY SYMBOLISM

143 United States of America, 1836 (Gobrecht)
(p. 197), 144 Great Britain, 1860 (L. C. Wyon)
(p. 196 f.)

A CENTURY OF ENGLISH QUEENLY PORTRAITURE

145
146 145 Victoria (W. Wyon) (p. 197), 146 Victoria (L. C. Wyon)
147 (p. 196 f.), 147 Elizabeth II (Mary Gillick) (p. 203 f.)

as witness Jan Pieters' beautifully proportioned and deeply felt compositions recording the Dutch floods of 1953 and the completion of repairs to the dykes.

Fifty years ago such technique and such originality in design would have been unthinkable. Today medallic design, as an art, is growing in strength and variety. If the world's mints could show a ready flexibility in taste and a willingness to give to the public designs a little more adventurous than those which have been "official choice" in the past, and if they were prepared to control the extent to which artists are limited by mechanical processes, it might well be that a renaissance in medallic art could in time affect, improve and powerfully sustain the standard of design in coinage as well.

Some Notes on Books and Public Collections

1. BOOKS

A mass of literature has grown up round coins and medals. But it is not easy to select what is useful in displaying design and technique. Many books which are important historically are poorly illustrated, and many short articles which are well illustrated are tucked away in the pages of periodicals. No modern periodical is published which relates the art of coins and medals intimately with other arts: *Aréthuse* did so from 1924, but ceased publication in 1931. Until recently coins and medals were seldom photographed direct from the metal, and most illustrations are those of plaster casts taken from the originals. While this method of illustration is of value to the scholar, it often fails to suggest the essential liveliness of design on metal.

The general range of the literature is well shown by P. Grierson's *Coins and Medals: a select bibliography* (=*Helps for Students of History*, No. 56. London, 1954). From out of this range a few can be mentioned here. Selected GREEK coins are beautifully illustrated in the British Museum's *The Principal Coins of the Greeks* (London, 1932) and, more fully, in C. T. Seltman's *Greek Coins* (London, 1933): the same author's *Masterpieces of Greek Coinage* (Oxford, 1949) employs welcome direct photography. Far more extensive in their scope are E. Babelon's *Traité des monnaies grecques et romaines* (Paris, 1907–32: only Greek coins were in fact covered), the British Museum Catalogues of Greek coins (29 volumes from 1873, by various authors), and the *Sylloge Nummorum Graecorum*, of which the British volumes run from 1931 and the Danish from 1942.

The enormous mass of ROMAN coinage has so far made it virtually impossible to produce a selectively illustrated yet helpful short survey, H. Mattingly's *Roman Coins* (London, 1928) being the best attempt. The same author's British Museum Catalogues of coins of the Roman Empire (1923–50) cover the ground from 31 B.C. to A.D. 222 in full detail. C. H. V. Sutherland's *Coinage in*

Roman Imperial Policy (London, 1951) illustrates many coins of the early Empire; M. Bernhart's much larger *Handbuch zur Münzkunde der römischen Kaiserzeit* (Halle, 1926) selectively illustrates the whole period of the Empire. Roman medallions are sumptuously reproduced in F. Gnecchi's *I Medaglioni romani* (Milan, 1912). Celtic design in western coinage can be enjoyed to the full in the superb direct-photography plates of L. Lengyel's *L'Art Gaulois dans les Monnaies* (Montrouge-Seine, 1954): R. P. Mack's *The Coinage of Ancient Britain* (London, 1953) illustrates (less dramatically) the parallel idiom in Britain.

The confusion into which Europe fell after the collapse of Rome has made it difficult to give similar broad classification to POST-CLASSICAL AND MEDIEVAL coinages, except in the case of Italy, where the great *Corpus Nummorum Italicorum*, in 29 volumes (Rome, 1910–40) based on the collection of the late King of Italy, gives a full range. Great masses of material are of course illustrated in the British Museum Catalogues of Byzantine (1908), Vandal (1911), and Anglo-Saxon coins (1887–93). In general, however, illustration of coins of this period is best sought in the immense number of sale catalogues published by dealers in England and abroad over many years past. The quality of the reproductions is often exquisite, and the range of their material immense.

With MODERN COINS, too, the same situation prevails. G. C. Brooke's *English Coins* (3rd ed., London, 1950) and E. Burns's *The Coinage of Scotland* (Edinburgh, 1887) cover Great Britain excellently, but continental coins, enormous in their variety, have not been in any way condensed by means of fine and selective illustration. W. Raymond's *Coins of the World: 19th century issues* (N.Y., 1947) and *20th century issues* (4th ed., N.Y., 1951) do something to cover the later material, assisted by J. S. Davenport's *European Crowns since 1800* (Buffalo, 1947) and *German Talers since 1800* (Galesburg, 1949). Modern technical processes are carefully considered in Sir John Craig's *The Mint* (Cambridge, 1953).

An excellent short introduction to MEDALS is J. Babelon's *La Médaille et Les Médailleurs* (Paris, 1927). The Italian Renaissance is magnificently illustrated in G. F. Hill's *A Corpus of Italian Medals of the Renaissance before Cellini* (London, 1930): the same author's *Pisanello* (London, 1905) and C. von Fabriczy's *Italian Medals* (Engl. transl., London, 1904) are also valuable. Hill's *Medals of the*

Renaissance (Oxford, 1920) dealt, besides Italy, with Germany, France and other countries. France, down to modern times, is well treated by J. Babelon's small *La Médaille en France* (Paris, 1948). The English medal down to the death of George II is lavishly pictured in *Medallic Illustrations of the History of Great Britain and Ireland* by E. Hawkins (ed. A. W. Franks and H. A. Grueber; London, 1885, 1904–11). L. Forrer's great *Biographical Dictionary of Medallists* (London, 1902–30) is indispensable.

2. PUBLIC COLLECTIONS

The Department of Coins and Medals at the British Museum houses one of the greatest collections in the world. Access to this, as to other public collections at home and abroad, is granted to those who are pursuing *bona fide* studies. At Oxford the Ashmolean Museum contains the oldest public collection in Great Britain: designed to serve the purposes of teaching, like that in the Fitz-william Museum at Cambridge, it is extremely large and repre-sentative. In Glasgow the Hunterian Museum contains the mag-nificent collection originally formed privately by Dr. William Hunter, while the National Museum and the Royal Scottish Museum at Edinburgh also possess strong collections.

Abroad there are many famous collections of outstanding quality and importance, often derived from those which were privately formed, on sumptuous lines, by kings and princes from the sixteenth to the eighteenth century. Of these it would be right to mention Paris, Munich, Rome, Vienna and Copenhagen as being perhaps specially rich (the fate of the renowned Berlin collection since the second world war remains obscure). Across the Atlantic a fine and famous collection exists in New York.

Outside the world's great public collections coins and medals are to be found, in relative abundance, in the stock of professional dealers and in auction-sales. The market is widespread in Europe, London being (as it has long been) one of its foremost centres.

Key to the Plates

(Note: Those instances in which photographs have been made from fine electrotypes, and not from the originals, are indicated by an asterisk.)

Frontispiece. CHARLES II of England (1660–1685), silver. Pattern "Petition" Crown by Thomas Simon. Scale 3:1. Ashmolean Museum.

1 ERETRIA (Euboea), silver. Octopus. Early fifth century B.C. Scale 2:1. British Museum.*

2 RHEGIUM (Italy), silver. Lion's mask. *c.* 460 B.C. Scale 1½:1. British Museum.*

3 METAPONTUM (Italy), silver. Ear of barley. *c.* 520 B.C. Scale 2¼:1. Ashmolean Museum.

4 ATHENS, silver. Owl, olive spray, crescent moon. *c.* 450 B.C. Scale 1½:1. E. S. G. Robinson. [See also No. 6 for obverse of same coin.]

5 ELIS (Peloponnese), silver. Eagle's head above leaf. By Da...... *c.* 420 B.C. Scale 2:1. Ashmolean Museum.

6 ATHENS, silver. Athena in crested helmet. *c.* 450 B.C. Scale 1½:1. E. S. G. Robinson. [See also No. 4 for reverse of same coin.]

7 SYRACUSE (Sicily), silver. Dolphins round head of Arethusa. *c.* 479 B.C. Scale 1½:1. British Museum.* [See also No. 22 for obverse of this coin.]

8 SYRACUSE (Sicily), silver. Arethusa. *c.* 440 B.C. Scale 2:1. British Museum.*

9 SYRACUSE (Sicily), silver. Arethusa. *c.* 450 B.C. Scale 2:1. Munich.

10 AETNA (Sicily), silver. Silenus. *c.* 470 B.C. Scale 2:1. Brussels.*

11 NAXOS (Sicily), silver. Dionysus. *c.* 460 B.C. Scale 1½:1. British Museum.*

12 AENUS (Thrace), silver. Hermes in close cap. *c.* 460 B.C. Scale 2:1. Munich.

13 AMPHIPOLIS (Macedon), silver. Apollo. *c.* 400 B.C. Scale 2:1. British Museum.*

14 CATANA (Sicily), silver. Apollo. By Heracleidas. *c.* 415 B.C. Scale 2:1. British Museum.*

15 ACANTHUS (Macedon), silver. Lion devouring bull. *c.* 400 B.C. Scale 2:1. E. S. G. Robinson.

16 TARENTUM (Italy), silver. Taras riding dolphin over sea. *c.* 450 B.C. Scale 2¼:1. Ashmolean Museum.

17 SYBRITA (Crete), silver. Hermes in wide hat. *c.* 360 B.C. Scale 2:1. British Museum.

215

18 GELA (Sicily), silver. Victory crowning river-god. *c.* 450 B.C. Scale 2:1. British Museum.

19 PEPARETHUS (island off Thessaly), silver. Running winged figure. *c.* 500 B.C. Scale 1½:1. British Museum.*

20 GELA (Sicily), silver. Young river-god. *c.* 440 B.C. Scale 1⅓:1. Ashmolean Museum.

21 SYRACUSE (Sicily), silver. Victorious four-horse chariot. By Euaenetus. *c.* 411 B.C. Scale 2:1. Ashmolean Museum.

22 SYRACUSE (Sicily), silver. Victorious two-horse chariot. *c.* 479 B.C. Scale 1½:1. British Museum.* [See also No. 7 for reverse of this coin.]

23 ACRAGAS (Sicily), silver. Apollo as sun-god in chariot. *c.* 410 B.C. Scale 1½:1. Munich.* [See No. 24 for reverse of this coin.]

24 ACRAGAS (Sicily), silver. Two eagles with captured hare. *c.* 410 B.C. Scale 1½:1. Munich.* [See No. 23 for obverse of this coin.]

25 PANTICAPAEUM (Tauric Chersonese), gold. Satyr. *c.* 360 B.C. Scale 2:1. British Museum.

26 CYZICUS (Mysia), electrum. Old man, wreathed. *c.* 350 B.C. Scale 3:1. British Museum.*

27 PHARNACES of Pontus, silver. *c.* 185–169 B.C. Scale 2:1. Paris.

28 MITHRADATES of Pontus, silver. *c.* 220–185 B.C. Scale 2:1. British Museum.*

29 ANTIOCHUS I of Syria, silver. 280–260 B.C. Scale 2:1. Ashmolean Museum.

30 TISSAPHERNES of Persia, silver. Early fourth century B.C. Scale 2:1. British Museum.*

31 BAGADAT of Persis, silver. Third century B.C. Scale 1½:1. British Museum.*

32 ANTIMACHUS of Bactria, silver. *c.* 190 B.C. Scale 1½:1. British Museum.*

33 PHILIP II of Macedon, gold. Apollo. 359–336 B.C. Scale 2:1. Ashmolean Museum.

34 NORTHERN GAUL, gold. "Apollo" head. *c.* 100 B.C. Scale 1½:1. British Museum.*

35 BRITAIN, gold. Celtic pattern from "Apollo" head. *c.* 50 B.C. Scale 1½:1. Ashmolean Museum.

36 ROMAN REPUBLIC, silver. The king Titus Tatius. *c.* 90–79 B.C. Scale 2:1. Ashmolean Museum.

37 ROMAN REPUBLIC, silver. The tribune Antius Restio. *c.* 54–44 B.C. Scale 2:1. Ashmolean Museum.

38 ROMAN REPUBLIC, silver. The consul Coelius Caldus. *c.* 78–55 B.C. Scale 2½: 1. Ashmolean Museum.

39 ROMAN REPUBLIC, silver. Bearded enemy (? Vercingetorix). *c.* 54–44 B.C. Scale 3:1. Ashmolean Museum.

40 ROMAN REPUBLIC, silver. Julius Caesar. *c.* 44 B.C. Scale 2:1. Ashmolean Museum.

41 ROMAN REPUBLIC, silver. Mark Antony. *c.* 41 B.C. Scale 2:1. Ashmolean Museum.

42 ROMAN REPUBLIC, silver. Pompey. *c.* 42–38 B.C. Scale 2:1. Ashmolean Museum.

43 AUGUSTUS, gold. 27 B.C.–A.D. 14. Scale 2:1. Phot. H. A. Cahn. [See No. 44 for reverse of this coin.]

44 AUGUSTUS, gold. Heifer. 27 B.C.–A.D. 14. Scale 2:1. Phot. H. A. Cahn. [See No. 43 for obverse of this coin.]

45 CLAUDIUS I, brass. A.D. 41–54. Scale 1½:1. Ashmolean Museum.

46 NERO, brass. A.D. 54–68. Scale 1½:1. Ashmolean Museum.

47 GALBA, gold. A.D. 68–69. Scale 2:1. Ashmolean Museum.

48 TIBERIUS, brass. Twin grandsons on horns of plenty. A.D. 14–37. Scale 1½:1. Ashmolean Museum. [See No. 49 for reverse of this coin.]

49 TIBERIUS, brass. Titles of his son Drusus. A.D. 14–37. Scale 1½:1. Ashmolean Museum. [See No. 48 for obverse of this coin.]

50 GALBA, brass. Emperor addressing troops. A.D. 68–69. Scale 1½:1. Ashmolean Museum.

51 HADRIAN, brass. A.D. 117–138. Scale 1½:1. Ashmolean Museum.

52 HADRIAN, brass (medallion). Half-length portrait. A.D. 117–138. Scale 1:1. Paris.

53 ANTONINUS PIUS, brass (medallion). A.D. 138–161. Scale 1:1. British Museum.

54 ANTONINUS PIUS, brass (medallion). Ship, river and bridge. A.D. 138–161. Scale 1:1. Paris.

55 COMMODUS, brass (medallion). The emperor as Hercules. A.D. 176–192. Scale 1½:1. British Museum. [See No. 56 for reverse of this medallion.]

56 COMMODUS, brass (medallion). The emperor as Hercules, with Nemean lion. A.D. 176–192. Scale 1½:1. British Museum. [See No. 54 for obverse of this medallion.]

57 CARACALLA, brass. A.D. 198–217. Scale 1½:1. Ashmolean Museum.

58 POSTUMUS, gold. A.D. 258–268. Scale 2:1. British Museum.

59 CONSTANTIUS I (Caesar), gold (medallion). A.D. 294–305. Scale 1:1. Arras.* [See No. 60 for reverse of this medallion.]

60 CONSTANTIUS I (Caesar), gold (medallion). Constantius rides into London. A.D. 294–305. Scale 1:1. Arras.* [See No. 59 for obverse of this medallion.]

61 DIOCLETIAN, gold (medallion). A.D. 284–305. Scale 1:1. British Museum.

62 CONSTANTINE THE GREAT, gold (medallion). "Praying" head. A.D. 307–337. Scale 1:1. New York.

63 CONSTANTINE THE GREAT, gold. Haloed head. A.D. 307–337. Scale 3:1. Ashmolean Museum.

64 CONSTANTIUS II, copper. A.D. 337–361. Scale 1½:1. Ashmolean Museum.

65 THEODAHAD (Ostrogoth), copper. A.D. 534–536. Scale 2:1. British Museum.

66 THEODORIC (Ostrogoth), gold. A.D. 493–526. Scale 1½:1. Rome.*

67 LONDON (?Bp. Mellitus), gold. *c.* A.D. 604–616. Scale 3:1. Ashmolean Museum.

68 OFFA OF MERCIA, silver. By Eadhun. A.D. 757–796. Scale 2:1. British Museum.

69 OFFA OF MERCIA, silver. "Pattern" obverse. By Eadberht. A.D. 757–796. Scale 2:1. British Museum.

70 UNCERTAIN ANGLO-SAXON, silver. Man with cup (of London style?). Eighth century. Scale 3:1. British Museum.

71 HALBERSTADT (Germany), silver. Stoning of St. Stephen. Twelfth century. Scale 1½:1. Phot. H. A. Cahn.

72 ERFURT (Germany) silver. St. Martin and Archbishop. Twelfth century. Scale 1½:1. Phot. H. A. Cahn.

73 HALBERSTADT (Germany), silver. St. Stephen entombed. Twelfth century. Scale 1:1. Phot. H. A. Cahn.

74 NORDHAUSEN (Germany), silver. Abbess kneeling to St. Eustace. Twelfth century. Scale 2:1. Phot. H. A. Cahn.

75 HERACLIUS, gold. Emperor and son. A.D. 610–641. Scale 2:1. British Museum.

76 JUSTINIAN II, gold. A.D. 685–695. Scale 2:1. Ashmolean Museum.

77 JUSTINIAN II, gold. Naturalistic portrait of Christ. A.D. 685–695. Scale 2:1. British Museum.

78 JUSTINIAN II, gold. Formal portrait of Christ. A.D. 685–695. Scale 2:1. Ashmolean Museum.

79 LEO III, gold. A.D. 717–741. Scale 2:1. British Museum.

80 CONSTANTINE VI, gold. A.D. 780–797. Scale 2:1. British Museum.

81 JOHN I ZIMISCES, gold. Virgin crowning emperor. A.D. 969–976. Scale 2:1. British Museum.

82 CHARLES I OF ANJOU, gold. 1266–1285. Scale 2:1. Phot. H. A. Cahn.

83 GIANFRANCESCO GONZAGA of Mantua (1407–1444), lead. Medal by Pisanello. Scale 1:1. British Museum.

84 The reverse of No. 83.

85 LEONELLO D'ESTE of Ferrara (1441–1450), bronze. Medal by Pisanello. Scale 1:1. Ashmolean Museum.

86 The reverse of No. 85.

87 DOMENICO MALATESTA of Cesena (1429–1465), lead. Medal by Pisanello. Scale 1:1. British Museum.

88 The reverse of No. 87.

89 ANTONY, BASTARD OF BURGUNDY (1421–1504), bronze. Medal by Candida. Scale 1:1. Ashmolean Museum.

90 GIOVANNI II BENTIVOGLIO of Bologna (1462–1509), bronze. Pattern for testoon by Francesco Francia. Scale 2:1. British Museum.

91 LOUIS XII of France (1498–1515), gold. Anonymous medal. Scale 1:1. Ashmolean Museum.

92 GIANGALEAZZO MARIA SFORZA of Milan (1476–1494), silver. Double ducat. Scale 2:1. Phot. H. A. Cahn.

93 LODOVICO MARIA SFORZA of Milan (1481–1500), silver. Double ducat. By Caradosso (?). Scale 1½:1. Ashmolean Museum.

94 GIANGALEAZZO MARIA SFORZA of Milan (1476–1494), silver. Double ducat. By Caradosso (?). Scale 1½:1. Ashmolean Museum.

95 CHARLES VIII of France (1483–1498), silver. Medal by Jean and Louis Lepère and Nicholas of Florence. Scale 1½:1. Ashmolean Museum.

96 The reverse of No. 95, with portrait of Anne of Brittany.

97 LOUIS XII of France (1498–1515), silver. Naples ducat. Scale 2:1. Phot. H. A. Cahn.

98 FERDINAND AND ISABELLA of Spain (1479–1506), gold. Doblon excellente. Scale 2:1. Ashmolean Museum.

99 HENRY VI of England (1422–1461), gold. Anglo-Gallic salut. Scale 2:1. Ashmolean Museum. (For reverse see No. 104.)

100 PHILIP IV of France (1285–1314), gold. Masse d'or. Scale 2:1. British Museum.

101 PHILIP VI of France (1328–1350), gold. Pavillon. Scale 2:1. Ashmolean Museum.

102 PHILIP VI of France (1328–1350), gold. Ecu d'or. Scale 2:1. British Museum.

103 The reverse of No. 109.

104 The reverse of No. 99.

105 The reverse of No. 110.

106 HENRY I of England (1100–1135), silver. Penny. Scale 2:1. British Museum.

107 EUSTACE FITZJOHN under STEPHEN of England (1135–1154), silver. Penny. Scale 3:1. Ashmolean Museum.

108 THE BLACK PRINCE under EDWARD III of England (1327–1377), gold. Anglo-Gallic hardi. Scale 2:1. British Museum.

109 EDWARD III of England (1327–1377), gold. Anglo-Gallic guiennois. Scale 2:1. British Museum.

110 EDWARD III of England (1327–1377), gold. Noble. Scale 2:1. Ashmolean Museum.

111 HENRY VII of England (1485–1509), gold. Sovereign. Scale 2:1. Ashmolean Museum.

112 The reverse of No. 111.

113 EDWARD III of England (1327–1377), silver. Groat. Scale 2:1. Ashmolean Museum.

114 JAMES IV of Scotland (1488–1514), silver. Groat. Scale 2:1. British Museum.

115 HENRY VII of England (1485–1509), silver. Shilling. Scale 2:1. British Museum.

116 EDWARD VI of England (1547–1553), gold. Pattern crown. Scale 2:1. Ashmolean Museum.

117 ELIZABETH I of England (1558–1603), gold. Pound. Scale 2:1. Ashmolean Museum.

118 The reverse of No. 117.

119 ELIZABETH I of England (1558–1603), copper. Pattern groat (?). Scale 1½:1. Ashmolean Museum.

120 JAMES VI of Scotland (1567–1603), gold. Ducat. Scale 2:1. Ashmolean Museum.

121 JAMES VI of Scotland (1567–1603), gold. Twenty-pound piece. Scale 1½:1. Ashmolean Museum.

122 JAMES VI of Scotland (1567–1603), gold. Hat piece. Scale 2:1. Ashmolean Museum.

123 CHARLES I of England (1625–1649), silver. Half-crown by Briot. Scale 1¼:1. Ashmolean Museum.

124 CHARLES I of England (1625–1649), gold. Three-pound piece (by Briot?). Scale 1:1. Ashmolean Museum.

125 The reverse of No. 124.

126 CHARLES I of England (1625–1649), silver. Pattern Oxford crown by Thomas Rawlins. Scale 1¼:1. Ashmolean Museum.

127 JOHAN-GEORG I of Saxony (1615–1656), silver. Thaler. Scale 1:1. Ashmolean Museum.

128 PETER I of Russia (1689–1725), silver. Rouble. Scale 1:1. Ashmolean Museum.

129 JOSEPH I of Hungary (1705–1711), silver. Double thaler. Scale 1:1. Ashmolean Museum.

130 LOUIS XIII of France (1610–1643), silver. Half écu. Scale 1¼:1. Ashmolean Museum.

131 POPE INNOCENT XII (1691–1700), silver. Scudo by G. Hamerani. Scale 1¼:1. Ashmolean Museum.

132 COSIMO III of Leghorn (1670–1723), silver. Pezza della rosa. Scale 1¼:1. Ashmolean Museum.

133 LOUIS XIV of France (1643–1715), silver. Ecu. Scale 1:1. Ashmolean Museum.

134 OLIVER CROMWELL of England (1653–1658), silver. Crown by Thomas Simon. Scale 1¼:1. Ashmolean Museum.

135 ANNE of England (1702–1714), copper. Pattern for halfpenny. Scale 1¼:1. Ashmolean Museum.

136 UNITED STATES OF AMERICA, copper. 1793 cent by Droz. Scale 1¼:1. Ashmolean Museum.

137 NAPOLEON BONAPARTE of France (Consul 1799–1804), silver. 5-franc piece by Tiolier. Scale 1¼:1. Ashmolean Museum.

138 CHARLES XIV of Sweden (1818–1844), copper. 1-skilling piece. Scale 1¼:1. Ashmolean Museum.

139 LOUIS NAPOLEON of Holland (1806–1810), silver. 50-stuiver piece by George. Scale 2:1. British Museum.

140 GEORGE III of England (1760–1820), silver. Crown by Pistrucci. Scale 1¼:1. Ashmolean Museum.

141 The reverse of No. 140.

142 GEORGE IV of England (1820–1830), gold. Sovereign by W. Wyon after Chantrey. Scale 2:1. Ashmolean Museum.

143 UNITED STATES OF AMERICA, silver. 1836 dollar by Gobrecht. Scale 2:1. British Museum.

144 VICTORIA of England (1837–1901), bronze. 1860 Penny by L. C. Wyon. Scale 1¼:1. Ashmolean Museum.

145 VICTORIA of England (1837–1901), silver. Pattern "Gothic" crown by W. Wyon. Scale 2:1. Ashmolean Museum.

146 The obverse of No. 144.

147 ELIZABETH II of England (1952–   ), cupro-nickel. Half-crown by Mary Gillick. Scale 2:1. Ashmolean Museum.

INDEX

The numerals in **heavy** type denote the *figure numbers* of the illustrations.

219